THE HISTORY OF THE UNITED KINGDOM

History Nerds

CONTENTS

Title Page	1
Introduction	5
Chapter 1 – Prehistoric Britain	6
Chapter 2 – "More deadly than these, the Romans"	16
Chapter 3 – King Alfred the Great	23
Chapter 4 –The King's Death Avenged: The Danes, the Normans, the English Earls and the Rebellious So	29
Chapter 5 – The Angevins	36
Chapter 6 – "Great Pits with the Multitude of the Dead"	45
Chapter 7 – The Tudor Rose without Thorns	54
Chapter 8 – The Last Tudor: "I Have a Lion's Heart"	63
Chapter 9 –The Early Stuarts	70
Chapter 10 – The Plague, the Fire and Conspiracies	79
Chapter 11 – "Carry the Lad that's Been Born to be King"	87
Chapter 12 –The Victorian Era	92
Chapter 13 – Britain at War	101
Chapter 14 – The United Kingdom: Post-War Challenges	111
Chapter 15 – Where Are the Weapons?	117
Conclusion –	120
Afterword	121

INTRODUCTION

The United Kingdom is a land of mystery steeped in legends of heroes such as King Arthur, Robin Hood King Alfred, Robert Bruce, and the heroes of the great seas. It was the British who defeated the so-called invincible Spanish Armada.

In the early days, the ancient Roman Empire was halted halfway through the island at Scotland. The British people are a collage of cultures descendant from the hardy Anglo-Saxons, the Normans, the Irish, the Welsh and the Picts.

Britain has yielded such figures as Sir Walter Raleigh, and poets such as Sir Walter Scott and playwrights such as William Shakespeare – all of whom have the alluring quality that attracts people of today who have jealously cherished their works – works and feats that will forever affect the history of humanity.

For years, the scholars have written histories and novels about the War of the Roses between the great houses of Lancaster and York. Much is written about Winston Churchill, the elegant queen, Elizabeth I, and the "Iron Lady," Margaret Thatcher, who was once quoted as scolding an American president, saying, "George, this it is no time to go wobbly!"

Do you wonder what it was that generated such mavens of prestige and integrity that is internally generated by a people who can never be defeated? Archeologists and ethnologists still seek to explain these mysteries. Buried in their history, the answers can be found and serve as a challenge to all who dare to imitate.

CHAPTER 1 – PREHISTORIC BRITAIN

The People Who Disappeared

Below is an elucidation of the people who were once in the British Isles and now are no more. They vanished, and were replaced, according to DNA studies. Were they victims of the mystical "hagstones" – stones with natural holes in them – which were used by the specters of hags that bewitched the first indigents of the British Isles – as an ancient myth predicted? Were these unfortunate settlers subject to a severe climactic change? Were they wiped out by half-crazed tribes that came in to rampage across their lands? Or, as Ian Amit, an archeologist from the University of Bradford conjectured, did they simply die out? That question beckon the question: "Why?"

Recent DNA studies have shown that there is a clear and distinct difference between the genetic patterns of the original Britons and Celts, and the following generations of people who settled in the British Isles. The first Britons simply "disappeared!" Scientists are bereft of an explanation as to what happened to the original Britons. Some anthropologists and archeologists say it happened during the Bell Beaker period. The "Bell Beaker" era was characterized by the presence of cup-like or vase-like pottery or the like. Many cultures had a bell beaker phase. The "beakers," or containers were used for drinking vessels and had flat bottoms. Initially they were quite plain, and sometimes were made of skulls.

There are widely disparate theories about the ethnic identity of the next wave of people who settled there. Some say that they had the lighter skin of the Caucasoid populations, thus resembling today's British people. Many have indicated that the Bell Beaker people originated with the Yamnaha culture in the eastern Steppes around the Caspian Sea. Yet others say the influx were the Saxons from Germanic roots. That probability is only rated as 54%. Yet another theory stems from legendary tales of ancient Troy.

Stonehenge

Stonehenge is a circular-shaped monument originally built around 3100 BCE. Its actual use has been and still is a subject of conjecture and controversy. Another mystery that spun off about Stonehenge indicates that the monument continued to be built and undated through 1600 BCE. The remains of 63 people were found there, though there are more likely more. The foundations for the standing stones were composed of chalk/flintstone bases and the stones themselves were of a type of sandstone called "sarcen." The configuration was of a ring of standing stones with stone lintels.

Later phases of the creation of Stonehenge were of "bluestone," an igneous rock with a bluish tinge. They were deliberately transported there from a great distance – from Carn Goedog and Craig Rhos-y-felin – about 140 miles west. The reason for bringing in the bluestones is lost in the silent history of the ancients.

The secondary purpose of Stonehenge is astronomical. The "heelstone" is a separate stone set apart from the ring. From the center of the circle, one can view the summer solstice rising directly over the heelstone, casting its rays straight through Stonehenge. There are similar astronomical configurations in other parts of the world such as in Karnak, Egypt.

Stonehenge and the Druids

Annually, the latter-day Druids conduct a ceremony at Stonehenge welcoming the sun and the moon of summer. According to the ancient historian, Pliny the Elder, the Druids of Gaul (ancient France) "were what they called their magicians – holding nothing more sacred than the mistletoe and a tree on which it is growing, provided it is a hard-timbered oak." Another mythological name for these people were the "oak men," mystical spirit people who populated the forests. The ancient Druids were known for their ancient ritual of welcoming the sixth day of the moon after the solstice by cutting mistletoe from an oak tree and sacrificing two white bulls. An elixir made from the mistletoe was used as a fertility potion for animals and a healing agent as well. Today, it is believed that the ancient oak men were Celts, not Gauls. During the Bronze Age Celts settled in parts of Gaul (France). They called their territory "Celica."

The "Legend" of Britain

According to the legend, the next wave of people who settled in Britain – the Caucasoid population – descended from the mythical soldier of Troy, Aeneas, circa 1250 BCE. According to legend told by the ancient chronicler, Geoffrey of Monmouth, Brutus, a descendant of Aeneas, tore through Aquitaine in Gaul and slaughtered many people of the tribes there. He had a vision of the great goddess Diana who spoke to him about a land beyond, which he named "Britannia":

> "Brutus, there lies beyond the Gallic bounds
> An island which the western sea surrounds,
> By giants possessed, now few remain
> To bar thy entrance...
> To raise a second Troy
> And found an empire in thy royal line."

Brutus and his companion, Corineus, "forced the giants to fly into the caves of mountains," then looked upon the island and noted its many rivers "abounding with fish." The potential existence of humanoid giants is written in the bible and their descendants were called "Nephilim."

In the ancient writings, it was said that Brutus built a "new Troy" upon the River Thames.

Bronze Age: Chalcolithic Era

This era arrived at different years in different places in Europe and the British Isles. It was estimated to have started in England around 2500 BCE, but may have overlapped the Neolithic Era in terms of the artifacts carbon-dated to that period. There is no clear consensus as to what years the next age, the Bronze Age spanned. The Chalcolithic Era was a time when copper was utilized to made weapons, shields and tools. Copper is made from native copper, tin, and sometimes lead. Those metals were were heated up in an oven and worked on a flat stone to achieve its shape. Notable was the manufacture of socketed axes, caldrons, socketed spearheads, axes, swords, helmets and horse bits. These were not merely plain, but had decorative elements on them – curves, circles, and vertical lines along the sword, probably identifying tribal membership and/or status.

Some large urns were used in their burial rituals. Remains were cremated during the Chalcolithic Era, placed into urns, covered and buried in chambers along with sentimental items, or insignias.

<u>The Urnfield Culture of the Bronze Age</u>

The Urnfield Culture arose at a time when the European and Eurasian societies became more advanced, and became involved in the building of villages and creating a social structure within their villages. Settlements were tailored to the geophysical conditions of the locale in which the people were building, and depended upon local resources.

There were fortifications built in the highlands and on hilltops built of stone and wooden ramparts. They consisted of a walled city or village surrounding dwellings which were houses with two or three aisles within. The walls were made of "wattle and daub." Wattles were wooden frameworks placed vertically or at angles if leading to a peak. The inner "walls" were composed of a mixture of clay, chalk dust, lime dust, dung and straw – the plaster of the day. Houses might also be round. Roofs were made of thatch, and were often whitewashed. That made it somewhat rainproof but also allowed for it to be painted with figures or designs on the internal walls.

Bronze Age Trade

Neighboring cultures started to trade items from their ships. In Dover, archeologists discovered what may have been one of the oldest ships of the Bronze Age. It was constructed of oak panels connected by wooden wedges and the planks were stitched together with Yew withies. A "withy" is a flexible branch like that of willow, used to tie one plank to the others. Two oarsmen could sit alongside each other on the horizontal benches. There was one sail, which, of course, was insufficient but did aid in creating propulsion.

Decoration on the weapons, scabbards, knives and helmets became more elaborate and attractive. Apparently the British exported a lot of tube sickles, which were sickles fashioned mostly from antlers, sheet metalwork. They imported more elaborate crested helmets to supplement the simpler ones they themselves designed. Most trade went on in the Mediterranean Sea, although England and Ireland could trade with each other, and goods could be brought back and forth from northern France and Spain. The trade was called Atlantic Bronze Age trade.

Britain and the Iron Age Tribes

The various ages of development hit different countries at different times, depending upon their contact with neighboring countries. In Britain, the Iron Age ran from about 800 BCE to 43 BCE.

In 350 BCE, a Greek explorer by the name of Pytheas traveled to England, which he called "Britannia." It was described by Pytheas and Diodorus, an historian of the 1st Century BCE, as being "subject to the Bear." Reference to the "Bear" had to do with the constellation Ursa Major in the northern sky. He added that the indigenous people there lived in thatched houses, grew grain and stored it in subterranean chambers.

Pytheas approached Britain by way of the Orkney Islands off its northern shore. In describing Pytheas's text, a later ancient geographer, Strabo, said that the people "live close to the frozen zone," and added that they consumed millet and roots. Pytheas traveled further south, disembarked and attempted to describe Stonehenge. He described the monument as a "Giants' Circle." The Atlantic Trade route that the British people had established died out for reasons unknown, so trade with countries across the Channel was limited. However, the Britons were subject to invasions, specifically from the Celts of Gaul.

Celtic Invasions

Warriors from the Parisi tribe of Celtica in Gaul stormed in, devastated the English farmlands in current-day Yorkshire and created their own fortified cities, called "oppida." These were massive settlements, surrounded by high stone walls which were guarded. The Celts remained in that area of England for years to come.

Chariot Burials

The Parisi's brought with them the practice of burying the whole body of a person, and the British thus discontinued cremation as the common practice. They also had the unusual custom of burying their warriors with their chariots and with their unfortunate chariot drivers as well. The chariots were disassembled and laid in an attractive design Some warriors were buried with their horses. Although the details are unknown, the drivers may have been slaughtered after the death of their lead warrior, out of respect – not a pleasant prospect indeed. These elaborate burials appear to have been used for the local elites of the villages.

Those who didn't have the distinction of being a member of a higher caste, were buried in long pits along with jars and goods donated by family members. For reasons unknown, their legs were bent up at the chest in a near-fetal position. One possible explanation might be that it allowed room for more bodies to be interred in larger cemeteries.

The Belgae

In northeastern Gaul, there was a tribe of people called the "Belgae." They were a violent people, who rushed into the British villages wild-eyed and greedy. The term "Belgae" is derived from an Old English root word, "bleigh," meaning "to swell or bulge," as if from anger.

Originally, the Belgae came from Germany, crossed the Rhine River and overran Gaul. They were fierce, and managed to keep neighboring war parties from the Teutonic, the Menapii and Cimbric tribes at bay. Moreover, they annihilated the Eburones, another tribe.

The Atrebates

Like the Belgae, the Atrebates fled Gaul and set up a colony in Southern England, right alongside that of the Belgae. Commius was their king in 30 BCE. He minted gold coins and had his image impressed upon them. The Atrebates were one of the most successful tribes in Britain. They had regular trade routes with mainland Europe, exchanging their finest product, textiles, as well as iron military equipment and armament, and hunting dogs for which they were well-known. Other tribes minted coins for the Romans who entered Britain around 55 BCE. It was a profitable pursuit.

The Cassivellauni

A Celtic tribe, the Cassivellauni settled in southern England in 20 BCE. Like the Atrebates before him, their King, Cassivellaunus, minted coins for the Romans. The Catuvellauni people were fortunate in that they settled just north of the River Thames, which was particularly fertile. He expanded his territory by encroaching on that of his neighbors, the Trinovantes to the east. Then he founded a new capital on the former Trinovantes land, calling it Camulodunum (today's Colchester).

The Druid of Colchester

In 1996, an ancient grave was unearthed near Colchester believed to have been that of a Druid. It was a chambered gravesite with a cremated body and a kit of medical instruments containing a medical probe, scalpels, a surgical saw and needles. Traces of mugwort, an aromatic plant were found. In ancient days, mugwort had medicinal benefits, serving as a primitive antibiotic. It also had psychological effects and was used as a relaxant – perhaps for those who were undergoing use of the surgical saw! The grave also had a fully intact board game which experts have been trying to fathom for years.

Dumnonii

This tribal territory is today the territory in which Devon, Exeter and Cornwall is located. It lay in the valley lowlands, and housed the future site of Roman baths. The term Domnu is an ancient mother goddess identified with the Celts. It is said that she was lured to the deep and overthrown by Tuatha de Danann. Tuatha is the head of the mystical fairy kingdom only spoken about by the Irish in whispers. In folklore he is associated with leprechauns and is a most powerful head of the fairy people. Dumnonii was named after a goddess named Domnu. She had great power, and, according to an Irish tale describes herself: "I am Domnu, the spirit that moves in the abyss. I am the bringer of life and bringer of death renewed...I am Mother of all."

The Durotiges

The Durotiges was a tribal nation of an assortment of Celtic tribes. The area actually dates back to Paleolithic times. There are about fifteen hill fortresses or castles there. The areas around Lambert's Castle, a hill fort in Dorset is noted for its greensand. Greensand is a unique type of sandstone, greenish in color, that flakes easily and was used by the ancient Britons as mortar because of its glauconite. Glauconite is a mineral naturally formed by decomposed marine life. Glauconite gives it a gritty texture and it was used for grinding as well.

The grasslands at Lambert's Castle are a virtual haven for botanists, as the area has one of the widest collections of grasses in the area.

The Trinovantes

The name "Trinovantes" was derived from a corruption of the name "New Troy," which was the original name the mythical founder of London called the capital city. London was settled on the north side of a tributary of the Thames River. The people who lived there were members of a vigorous and powerful tribe that came in after the ancient tribes. The Trinovantes and the Cassivelaunus were bitter enemies.

The Picts

The Pictish Confederation was formed from a combination of Iron Age tribes who, it was said, lived in the far north in England. Their origins are reportedly Celtic. According to several ancient historians, Bede the Venerable, Geoffrey of Monmouth, and Holinshed, they may have been the original conquerors. "They passed away from us, with the splendor of swiftness, to dwell by valor in the land of the country beyond Ile. From thence they conquered Alba, according to the ancients. "Alba" was an ancient term assigned to Britannia. At the time the Picts may have called themselves "Albidosi" after the land they claim they founded.

CHAPTER 2 – "MORE DEADLY THAN THESE, THE ROMANS"

The ancient historian, Tacitus, spoke through the mouths of the Britons in foreboding terms: "But now there are no people beyond us, nothing but tides and rocks and, more deadly than these, the Romans." The ancient Romans spoke about Britain with disdain, saying the weather was miserable, and there was frequent mists and rain. Apparently overlooking the fact that the Romans came charging in as invaders decked out in armor, spears and swords, they criticized the Britons for being fierce and inhospitable. The Britons dyed their skin with woad, which was a blue, or sometimes green dye, made from flowers that are dried and fermented.

In 55 BCE, Julius Caesar claimed that these Britons were aiding his enemies, the Gauls, and felt he could put an immediate stop to that. He and his legionnaires stormed into Kent, but he wasn't prepared to battle a great storm that blew up along the coast, and the invasion was postponed.

The early tribes were terrified at the arrival of the great Roman galley warships, called "long ships." They were huge and oar-driven, with oarsmen stacked two or three-high. In the center, each ship had one sail, and a "corvus," which was a ramp that could be lowered on to the deck of another ship or on shore.

On the following year, 54 BCE, Caesar returned with many legions of heavily armed warriors. The British tribes had weapons far inferior to his, so Caesar took full advantage of the shortcoming. They exchanged hostages, which was the custom at that time, and he guaranteed that he wouldn't ever attack those tribes who would pay him an annual tribute. Essentially, that was extortion. However, they did agree to the tribute and made a payment or two, but there is no record that they made any more once Caesar left.

Caesar was looked upon as a pseudo-savior, because a local king of the Cassivellauni tribe, Mandubracius, had been usurped from his throne by Cassivellaunus, and rushed to Caesar for help. It turned out, Caesar discovered that Cassivellaunus was a general and not the legitimate successor, so Caesar restored the throne to its rightful heir.

Although Caesar Augustus planned raids into Britain, weather interfered and he never set foot on its soil. Instead, Rome and Britain established a healthy trade. The next contact from Imperial Rome wasn't initiated until 43 CE when Emperor Claudius interceded for the benefit of Verica, the king of the Atrebates who had been falsely exiled.

The Iceni

When Roman Emperor, Claudius, invaded Britain in 43 CE, the Iceni tribe didn't take them on in battle. They made peace with them and agreed on sending hostages and payment of a tribute. They maintained good relations with the Romans, and even participated in minting coins for them. However, in the year 60 CE, the Romans who came in to collect their coins were abusive and crude. They looked down upon the Iceni with disdain. When Boudica, Queen of the Iceni, complained, they allegedly scourged her and raped her daughter.

Boudica's Rebellion

Boudica rose up, and allied herself with the Trinovantes tribe and some others, and rebelled. The conflict included not just men, but women warriors as well. Much to the shock of the Roman legions, they destroyed a Roman settlement at Camulodunum (Colchester). Rumours circulated that they slaughtered as many as 70,000 Roman soldiers, however, that was a gross exaggeration. In actuality, only several hundred Romans were killed.

The Emperor who succeeded Claudius, Nero Drusus, was incensed at the Roman defeat at those battles, and had his general Seutonius, regroup and defeated the Iceni. No one knows what happened to Boudica after that battle. Some say she committed suicide to avoid capture. She is remembered as the heroine of 1st Century Britannia.

The Caledonians

By the year 79 CE, Rome had control of southern England, including Wales. However, many fierce tribes had settlements north of there, specifically the Picts. Like many of the other Britons, they detested the rule of these overlords. The various regions of the south Britannia were assigned Roman governors, who insisted on being treated like kings and gave out orders at their whim.

The Caldonians and sometimes the Picts frequently raided the Roman colonies, devastating their farms and destroying their villages. The Caledonians, like many of the other tribes were of Celtic origin, but they were true Britons in heart and spirit. The ancient historian, Jordanes, described the Caledonians, saying they "have reddish hair and large loose-joined bodies." Today's Scots, perhaps?

Caledonians built hill fortresses and were vicious warriors, having beaten the Romans on numerous occasions. Many refugees from southern England fled north to join them and encouraged them to resist a further spread of Roman rule. There were several other smaller tribes who inhabited northern England – the Vacomagi, the Taexali and the Venicones – who needed their protection. The Votadini tribe, however, was also there, but had a long-standing agreement with Rome that kept them above the fray.

Hadrian's Wall

The Roman emperor at that time was Publius Aelius Hadrianus, or simply Hadrian. At that time there were rebellions even in southern Britain, as well. The emperor sent in Quintus Pompeius Falco to quell the rebellious Britons and restore order. Pompeius then told the emperor about the raids from the tribes to the north, specifically the Caledonians and the Picts. Hadrian, like the emperors before him, had no wish to expand British borders beyond those of southern England, so he contracted some of the people, even including Britons to build a formidable wall across Britain.

Hadrian's Wall was 73 miles across with forts interspersed called "milecastles." They were later manned by Roman legionnaires. Construction started in the year 122 CE and it took six more years to build. There were ditches on either side of the wall, which was very wide, and extra mounds to slow down an invading force. Forts were also put into place, manned by a number of soldiers. Sections of that wall still remain today and are a tourist attraction.

In an attempt to prevent even more invasions from the North, the following emperor, Antoninus Pius, built a wall further north in 142 CE, called the Antonine Wall, which was mostly a huge berm, but enhanced with Roman baths for the soldiers, who were, no doubt, bored from hours of vigilance, waiting for an invasion which may or may not come. Antoninus felt this wall would be more of a symbol of the great power of
the Roman Empire.

As the Roman Empire started to decline, so did the Antonine Wall and it fell into disuse twenty years later. Little by little, Roman settlements in Britannia were abandoned. The wood gave into the ravages of weather, and only portions of stone walls remained as the Roman Empire slid in its downward cycle toward its bitter end which occurred in 476 CE.

Collapse of the Economic System

After the Romans left, Britain lacked the organization imposed by the Romans. Therefore, they reverted to their former ways. Coinage was no longer used, as the Romans weren't there to purchase it, and that lowered everyone's income. Archaeologists reported finding the old Roman coins with holes in them, indicating that the people started to use them as jewelry. Town life changed; buildings were abandoned as the Roman settlement emptied out. It was depressing, but that was interrupted by new threats.

New Invasions Replace Roman Occupation

Open fields and abandoned Roman farms lay fallow, inviting raids from barbarian tribes, most of whom came from the Germanic provinces and included the Angles, Saxons and Frisians. In the smaller towns, class struggles erupted among the Britons, as they lacked cohesive leadership. Britain was fragmenting into smaller kingdoms where tyrants, as well as good kings ruled their limited regions. These so-called "kings" were actually warlords – men with good native military skills accustomed to leading other men, either for good or ill.

One such chieftain was Vortigern. He was called a tyrant by his contemporaries, but did manage to organize forces to fight off the Picts and Scots from raiding the lands in southern England, despite the Antonine and Hadrian Walls. Vortigern's own men rebelled against him, as he became more avaricious and careless in his rule. His men then settled in what is now called Kent, and Vortigern, so the ancients state, fled from place to place, finally ending up in Wales.

According to the historian, Gildas, those were dark days permeated with more disturbances, some of which were caused by the new chieftains of the old tribes, again raising themselves up to dominate the people Gildas wrote in his tome, *On the Ruin of*

Britain, "Britain is a land fertile with tyrants."

Arthurus: The Glorious King Arthur

Much controversy surrounds the accuracy of a story about an historical hero named King Arthur, but history actually *does* record the existence of a hero named Arthurus. An 18th Century archeologist, William Stukeley, claimed to have found artifacts from Arthur's legendary kingdom of Camelot, which was also associated with a fort named Camulodunman in Somerset.

People loved King Arthur, although many doubted his existence. Even the 15th Century contemporary historians like Polydore Virgil indicated that King Arthur's story was a myth. That angered another 17th Century scholar, Edward Littleton, who said: "What have we to do with Polydore Virgil? One Virgil was a poet, and the other a liar."

King Arthur's appearance lit up the gloomy days of the 5th or 6th Century when Rome left. His story has been told and retold by minstrels along with exaggerated stories in ancient history when chroniclers editorialized their work. This was work done, not in vain, but as means to raise the hopes of a people buried in chaos and conflict. During those chaotic days, the Saxons and other half-crazed barbarians swarmed all over Britain, attacking them at every opportunity.

Arthur at the Battle of Mount Badon

Circa 500 or possibly 560 CE, the twelfth battle of the wars with the Anglo-Saxons occurred in southwestern Britain, when the ferocious and bloodthirsty Anglo-Saxons first "dipped their red and savage tongues in the western ocean," according to Gildas. Another contemporary historian, Nennius, spoke of the same battle, saying that "there fell in one day 960 men from one charge by Arthur, and no one struck them down except Arthur himself!" One can see Nennius's hyperbole, but it was for good cause. They said that Arthur brought an insignia of the Virgin Mary with him and carried his sword, which he called "Caliburnus," Medieval

Latin for "Excalibur." Other accounts cited that he killed just 470 mean – an overwhelming amount at any rate.

Arthurian tales were related in the ancient Anglo-Saxon Chronicle that Arthur slayed Ceawlin, the Anglo-Saxon king of the newly-established kingdom of Wessex.

Wars Throughout the Centuries

While the Britons fought the Anglo-Saxons, the Picts and Scots in the north descended upon the territories in the south. Over the course of two centuries, the Anglo-Saxons settled in Essex, Wessex, Mercia and East Anglia in the midlands, Sussex and Kent. The Frisians, mentioned early, represented just a fraction of the people and intermingled with the Anglo-Saxons in Kent. The Frisians were once mostly mercenary soldiers for the Romans and many returned to the Germanic areas from which they migrated.

Mostly, the Anglo-Saxons, though, clustered their settlements to the east of the British Isles, while the Britons lived along the western shores. Areas of Northumberland were also settled by the Anglian people, but it was more fully occupied by the Anglo-Saxons.

CHAPTER 3 – KING ALFRED THE GREAT

After Rome left the British Isles, Cedric became the founder of a long line of Anglo-Saxon Kings. He was the monarch of Wessex, or the current-day Hampshire. He was descendant from King Cerdic, whom King Arthur reportedly slaughtered at the Battle of Mount Baden possibly around 534 CE.

Cerdric was a pagan worshipper of Woden also known as "Odin," the chief god most commonly associated with Norse mythology these days. Odin was a mysterious figure of legend with magical powers of healing and the ability to wield the spirits of the night to do his bidding. At night, he led the ghostly parade of the long since dead accompanied by an army of angelic beings called "Valkyries" across the night sky. He slayed the primordial beast of the underworld, and was also the god of the Norsemen. (Vikings) Their god, Woden, it was believed, developed the runic alphabet. The heavenly world he lorded over is the legendary Valhalla.

Christianity comes to Britain

Between the 5th and 6th Century CE, Augustine the Bishop of Hippo, in North Africa was tasked with the conversion of the Saxons. In the Anglo-Saxon Chronicle, it says that 596 CE was the year in which "Pope Gregory sent Augustine to Britain with many monks, to preach the word of God to the English people."

In 871 CE in Wessex, Alfred fought alongside his brother, Aethelred against the Vikings and their allies in Wessex. The entire island was them seriously threatened by the "Heathen

Army," the Danes allied with the Vikings. They already had possession of North Umbria. The Vikings, from Scandinavia, were traders by nature, and developed the uncanny ability to build great long ships with short keels, so as to navigate most rivers inland. The ships were light, and could be carried by the sailors over patches of land between tributaries. The Vikings were bloodthirsty and fearsome and used every kind of weapon imaginable – swords, bows and arrows, axes, lances and spears. In addition, they carried shields and wore chain mail and helmets.

The Battle of Ashdown 871 CE

The Vikings and Danes were a huge foraging party, and they rampaged through the countryside, killing people and animals and destroying the crops. The Saxons were defeated initially, but returned to have their revenge They had worked hard to keep their land and weren't going to let it go so easily. Unfortunately, at Ashdown, the Danes had the advantage, as they were uphill from the defenders. Fiercely, Alfred ascended step by step up the craggy slope. They came up in shield-wall formations – that is, when the soldiers stand closely side-by-side. That was, no doubt, a trick they learned from the Romans. Later, Alfred was followed up by his brother's force, who used the same tactic, which was most effective in picking off the survivors of the first attack. However, Aethelred died in the battle, and Alfred became king. The king of the Vikings, Bagsecg, was also killed. Whenever that happens, an army's soldiers can lose heart and fail to perform as effectively. The Viking earls were able to continue downward with the attack, but five of them were slaughtered leading to raised hopes for the Saxons, but it was short-lived, as they lost two succeeding battles and were forced to retreat to the marshes of Somerset. The Saxons then began to engage in guerilla warfare.

The Battle of Edington 878 CE

Unlike the Danes and Vikings, the Saxons understood the lowlands there. The armies under "Guthrum the Old," a weathered warrior, retreated to their earthen fort, Chippenham. From there the Danes staged a daring attack in an unexpected sudden strike, but it wasn't successful and they retreated back to Chippenham. The Saxons decided to just wait them out. When the Danes and Vikings were hit by the cold and hunger, they despaired and surrendered.

The Treaty of Wedmore

Alfred knew he couldn't expel all of the invaders out of Britain, so he made an agreement with Guthrum indicating that the Danes and Vikings could occupy certain large territories in the east and the northeast, but were to leave Wessex for the Saxons.

Alfred then constructed a chain of fortifications between the two kingdoms, calling the area of their opponents "Danelaw." The fortifications there were called "burghs."
The King then built garrisons that were manned all year round.

The Danes didn't keep to all the points in the treaty and it eventually had to renegotiated. In the end, which probably occurred around 879 CE, it is interesting to note that – as part of the agreement – Guthrum was baptized into the Christian faith with Alfred serving as his godfather.

The Battle of Cynwit

Despite the agreement between the Saxons and the Danes, there were still sporadic attacks. The Anglo-Saxon Chronicle and other ancient texts weren't very exact but it is believed that the two forces engaged each other near Somerset and at Countisbury Hill in Devon in 878 CE. This battle was led by Odda, the elderman of Devon, on behalf of the Saxons against Ubba, and the brother of the well-known warrior, "Ivar the Boneless." Much amusing discussion had been bandied around by historians as to the meaning of that nickname, and it was generally concluded that he was using a peg leg or peg legs, or – in a stretch of the imagination – it was conjectured that it meant he was impotent!

At any rate, Odda succeeded, killing Ubba and "eight hundred men" according to the Chronicle. The biggest victory lay in the fact that Odda was able to take possession of the flag of their army– a Raven. In those times taking the flag was a great prize with much meaning.

The Wessex Navy

Alfred was active all his life. In 880, Alfred built himself a small fleet, and two years later the Danes again attacked. According to the Anglo-Saxon Chronicle, the King "set out to sea with a fleet and fought with four ship rovers of the Danes, taking two of their ships, wherein all the men were slain and the other two (ships) surrendered."

Legacy

King Alfred didn't spend his whole life at war. He made solid contributions to his people. He wrote a system of laws, collected from the practices of the kings who served before him, and added his own. It had a section where he had the Ten Commandments, letters from the Acts of the Apostles, and excerpts from the Book of Exodus printed as well. Much of the Bible at that time was written in Latin, but he wanted it translated into English so the commoners could read it as well. To that book, he added his own exhortation telling his subjects that Christ "taught mercy and meekness." Alfred had always had an interest in justice with mercy.

He also had his learned men select books that all should know, then had them translated into English. The people were encouraged to read and study them. He set up a "Court School," which imparted education and also distributed books he felt that free men should learn in order to be successfully employed.

King Alfred died in 899 CE, but the manner of his death is unknown. It had been theorized that he suffered from Crohn's disease.

Aethelstan: King of the Anglo-Saxons

It wasn't until Alfred's grandson, Aethelstan took the throne, that England became unified. Aethelstan became king of what remained of Mercia, and his half-brother, Aelfweard, was the king of Wessex. Unfortunately, Aelfweard died soon after taking over Wessex, and, in 925 CE, Aethelstan was crowned king of both kingdoms. The jealous nobles objected to Aethelstan, and plots arose to blind him. That disability would have made him incapable of holding office, according to the British law at the time. It was a nefarious plot, possibly involving, Frithestan, the Bishop of Winchester. Frithestan resented Aethelstan, as he was the successor, but born illegitimately. Frithestan felt that the throne should have been awarded to Edwin, Aelfweard's younger brother. Often rivals for the throne murdered each other to seize kingships, but Frithestan – being a man of the cloth – perhaps decided that blinding the young man would make himself less culpable. The plot failed, but the bishop and Aethelstan remained enemies for years. The bishop didn't even attend the coronation ceremony, which was a highly insulting affront.

Invasion of Scotland

The issue became moot when Edwin died in a shipwreck in the North Sea. Some suspected that Edwin was deliberately drowned. Edwin's death ended any serious threats to Aethelstan assuming his place among the great and future kings of England. So, in 934 CE, Aethelstan invaded Scotland.

Little is said in the records about the battles in Scotland, but Aethelstan was accompanied by many Welsh princes and their troops. They marched through Nottingham, and northward, battling any forces that resisted them, and ravaging the lands as far north as Dunnoffar and Fortriu in the land of Picts. The texts indicate that he even reached Orkney. The lack of texts on the various battles led historians to conclude that he may have met little resistance. Aethelstan made Constantine II the king of

Scotland and Aethelstan became the supreme ruler of Wessex, Mercia and now Scotland.

Battle of Brunanburh 937 CE

This was one of the most significant battles in England prior to the Middle Ages. Aethelstan, the King of the Anglo-Saxons and his brother Edmund I, went up against powerful opposition – Olaf Guthfrithson, the King of Dublin; Owen I of Strathclyde (a portion of Scotland); and Constantine II of Scotland. Constantine II treacherously turned traitor against Aethelstan, as he was greedy for power for himself. This force was aided by the earls of those hostile lands, and hordes attacked the Britons.

Aethelstan, Edmund I and the combined forces of the Saxons of Wessex and Mercia confronted the enemies at Brunanburh. It was a long day's battle. According to the Anglo-Saxon Chronicle, "Pursuing fell the Scottish clans; the men of the fleet in numbers fell; midst the din of the field the warrior sweat...With chosen troops throughout the day, the West Saxons fierce pressed on the loathed bands." Thousands died, and history records that even fathers left their sons lying slain upon the battlefield: "Their sons, too, were left on the field of battle, mangled with wounds, young at the fight."

The Norsemen fled; and so too the Irish fighters from across the sea came home in disgrace. Constantine fled to Scotland and so did Owen who "departed in nailed ships." Kings from smaller sub-kingdoms from the North were slain: "Five kings lay on the field of battle, in the bloom of youth, pierced with swords."

Aethelstan had successfully prevented the fragmentation of England, although Scotland, Strathclyde and Northumbria preserved their independence.

CHAPTER 4 – THE KING'S DEATH AVENGED: THE DANES, THE NORMANS, THE ENGLISH EARLS AND THE REBELLIOUS SON

"Men Murdered Him"

In 978 CE, Edward, king of the Saxons, was slain. The Chroniclers say, "There has not been 'mid Angles a worse deed done that this was, since they first sought Britain-land." He was declared a martyr by the Catholic Church, the Orthodox Church and the Anglicans. Perhaps, more rightly, he was murdered by the scrambles that occur whenever a succession is questioned, as happened in this case.

Aethelred the Unready

The term "unready" meant "poorly advised." And he was.

After twenty years of peace, the ferocious Danes rose up again. In 991, the Britons were slaughtered brutally by the Danes at the Battle of Maldon. The beaten Britons were made to pay a hefty tribute in exchange for a peace that wasn't to last long before the Danes continued their attacks. They raided Devon, Cornwall, south Wales, western Somerset, Sussex, Hampshire, Dorset and Kent.

In 1001 CE, a fleet of swift Danish ships also came into Sussex and destroyed it. Aethelred was only able to defend the attack at Exeter. Foolishly, this "unready" king then kept paying tributes in exchange for peace, and the Danes were making a fortune.

Then Aethelred lost his temper.

St. Brice's Day Massacre 1002 CE

That year, King Aethelred passed an order to execute any Dane living in Britain! He said that they "were to be destroyed by a most just extermination, and thus this decree was to be put into effect even as far as death." The number of the slain wasn't recorded, but archeologists discovered the bones of about 35 young men, and forensic examination revealed that they had been repeatedly stabbed.

Among the victims was Gunhilde, the sister of Sweyn Forkbeard, the Danish king. In retaliation, Sweyn sacked Norwich, and more Danish forces attacked western Britain. The Anglo-Saxon commander, Ulfcytel, inflicted heavy losses upon the Danes, but the Saxons were finally defeated in 1005. The Danes then demanded more tribute money.

King for a Year

Sweyn returned and invaded yet again in 1013. The English defenses virtually collapsed and Aethelred fled to Normandy, France. Sweyn was then the King of England. Due to his subjects losing all confidence in Aethelred, many nobles swore allegiance to the Danish king. However, he died the following year. He was succeeded by Canute the Great.

Canute snapped up nearly all of Britain. In the meantime, the English nobles had Aethelred reinstated as king and he marched toward London to recapture it. Aethelred's son, Edmund Ironside, also lost faith in his father, and went to war using his own forces. Edmund fought brilliantly, and took possession of London, reconciling it with his father. Aethelred died in 1016 CE.

Edmund went to battle at Oxford, and Canute was defeated, but did win the battle of Assandun after that. The location of that battle is known today. There the Danes prevailed. In the end, Edmund and Canute decided that Edmund would retain Wessex, and Canute would take the rest of England. They further agreed that, if either one of them died, all of Britain would be the property of the one who survived.

Oddly enough, Edmund died later on in the same year as his father– 1016. England was then ruled by the Dane, Canute, and after him two more Danes, one of whom – Harthacnut. Harthacnut had a half-brother of English royal blood, Edward, later called Edward the Confessor. He was named such because of his piety. Even though he was called "pious," he was nevertheless suspected of poisoning Harthacnut, who died very suddenly in 1042 CE. Edward was then the King of England.

England was now back in English hands, though not for long. Edward the Confessor had no heirs, and it is said that he promised the kingdom to Harold Godwinson, an earl and faithful supporter. Suddenly, it was discovered that Edward the Confessor had a long-lost nephew, Edgar Aethling. Edgar, still a minor, was then taken to the palace.

Often there were scrambles over accession to the throne, so Duke William of Normandy in France, Edward's cousin once removed, also claimed the throne. Harold Godwinson, in the meantime, said that, since he had been asked to be king, he would take it and then hand throne over to Duke William. During the last days of Edward's life, it was believed that Harold decided to reneg on that secret promise so, Harold and William were both contenders for the throne.

Harold had the support of the Witan, the king's advisors and the noblemen of the realm, and he was crowned King of England. William assembled a massive force in Normandy and sailed to Pevensey in Southern England. Harold heard about his arrival and rushed his troops there to challenge William.

The Norman Conquest – The Battle of Hastings 1066 CE

Both sides had infantrymen, but Harold had more foot soldiers than archers. William, however, had not only infantrymen, but more arches that Harold had, and brought a swift cavalry with him. The English were in a close formation, and the Normans couldn't break through those lines. They then feigned retreat to tempt the other force to race toward them and cause them to break formation. When Harold and his forces charged forward, Williams' troops turned around suddenly to face them. William's archers moved to one side and shot out volleys of arrows. The battlefield eventually broke up into many skirmishes, going on all day until dusk.

As the shadows lengthened over the blood-soaked mud, those few who remained scattered from the fight. The field was strewn with thousands of dead warriors, piled one upon another. Upon one pile lay the body of King Harold.

The young nephew of Edward the Confessor, Edgar Aethling, was then the next in line for the throne, but was never crowned which marked the end of the Anglo-Saxon kings of England.

On Christmas Day, 1066, William of Normandy was crowned King of England. He kept Edgar Aethling at court until he was of age and William awarded him with a grant of land. The other earls who were there before Hastings continued in their positions as before, except for relatives of Harold Godwinson, William's nemesis.

All Was Not Well

In 1068, Earl Edwin of Mercia, Earl Morcar and Earl Gospatric- both of Northumbria – rebelled, complaining bitterly about their positions within Norman England. Edwin was incensed at the growing power of one of William's friends, William FitzOsbern, who arrived from Normandy and was immediately named the Earl of Wessex.
William's solution was unique. He traveled through the country building huge castles in the troubled lands.

All was still not well. Edward the Confessor's nephew, Edgar, had plans. He teamed up with the old Dane from the past – Sweyn Forkbeard – who came rushing over with his fleet. Together, they attacked York, Exeter and Shrewsbury. Gleeful at his victory at York, Edgar Aethling then had himself crowned king.

William reacted quickly. He bought off the Danes, who left, and Edgar fled to Scotland, taking refuge under the protection of King Malcom. William then charged up north to take care of Earls Edwin and Morcar. Earl Edwin was betrayed by his own men and slain, while Morcar was captured and imprisoned. In 1072, William attacked King Malcolm of Scotland, and the refugee, Edgar, fled to Flanders in France. William and Malcom signed a peace treaty.

In 1073, William, who was also the Duke of Normandy, then had to race back to Normandy to handle an invasion of the County of Maine by Fulk le Rechin, the Count of Anjou. He quickly defeated the Count. Edgar Aethling was there in Flanders, and to make matters worse William had another possible foe, Philip, the King of France. The unhappy Edgar, however, was forced to submit to William and he returned home to Britain.

The English Earls Revolt!

Now William was trying to rule two territories, Normandy and all of England. While he was in Normandy, the English earls took advantage of his absence. The Earl of Norfolk, Ralph de Gael, and the Earl of Hereford, Roger de Breteuil, revolted. The Earl of Northumbria, Waltheof, joined also. William, still in France, had his faithful troops put down the rebellion. Earl Ralph de Gael, however, was still trapped in Norwich Castle. The desperate earls then called out to the Danes to help. However, Williams warriors subdued the revolt. Roger and Waltheof were imprisoned. but Ralph de Gael escaped Norwich Castle and fled to Brittany in France where he owned some land.

After the defeat of the Earls, Canute, the Dane, arrived with as many as 200 ships. Since the Earls' revolt had been put down, the Danes seized the opportunity to raid some of the seaports along the British coast.

Ralph de Gael, the Earl who had fled home to Brittany, seized control of the castle at Doi in Brittany so William had his troops march over there to wrestle control back. Ralph de Gael defeated William and word of King William's first defeat raced around both France and England. In 1077, William was forced to make peace with the earls and unceremoniously went to Normandy.

The Rebellious Son

Robert Curthose was King William's arrogant son who had been living in Normandy. Robert and his brothers, William and Henry, often got into a childish arguments. It is believed that Robert and his siblings were spoiled. Robert first lead an insurrection against his father after a prank played by his brothers who emptied a chamber pot over his head. He brawled with his brothers which was subsequently interrupted by their father. In Robert's eyes his father had failed to punish his brothers causing Robert to storm away feeling his pride and dignity had been insulted. Robert then found a group of rowdy friends, and together they decided they would lead an insurrection against William and seize the castle at Rouen. When they failed in their attempt they fled to an ally before fleeing again when King William attacked their base at Remald. King William's enemies on the continent decided to join up with the boys. In the end father and son were brought to peace by the pleas of Robert's mother.

William as King

William created Royal forest lands out of confiscated estates, as he enjoyed hunting. He also created land holdings for many of the nobles who were loyal to him, including some of the French. He divided the country into shires run by sheriff and also had a book written, called the Domesday Book, carefully recording all the lands owned and by whom. It was for the purpose of tax collection, but also a way by which he could feel proud of his possessions. He was the largest landowner in all of England.

In 1087 CE, King William had an accident with his horse, and later died of the injury he received.

CHAPTER 5 – THE ANGEVINS

"Anjevin" is French for the term "from Anjou." England and Normandy were at war in 1135. Henry I ruled Anjou at the time, but died causing battles to erupt everywhere. Thousands were slain and anarchy prevailed. Empress Matilda and the king's cousin, Stephen of Blois, struggled over the throne. Matilda was able to gain control of southwest England, but was trapped by Stephen in Oxford Castle. That conflict echoed throughout the country. The barons of the many estates fought among each other. Welsh leaders rebelled as did the Scots. Mercenaries were hired by the various parties which added to the bloodshed. Anjou was in utter chaos.

Empress Matilda escaped by sneaking away all dressed in white as a camouflage in the snow fleeing to her native Normandy. The violence nevertheless continued until Stephen of Blois became the next king. Local wars among the landowners and barons continued throughout his reign.

Henry II

After Stephen's death, Henry II was crowned king in 1154 CE. He reduced the overbearing power of the barons and tried to restore land to those from whom it had been stolen during the war. He was a firm ruler who restored the honor of the monarchy.

Henry established a more cohesive set of laws, as the ones currently in force were characterized by overlapping jurisdictions. Ecclesiastical law and civil law weren't clearly distinct and he worked to correct that.

Having seen so much injustice when the barons went into armed conflict, snatching each other's estates and farmlands, he felt obligated to create a legal system that could right those wrongs. He placed capable administrators in charge of various districts, and his local courts, called "shire courts" decided land disputes.

In 1176, Henry established circuit courts, called "Eyres," which were run by traveling justices and court officials. They administered to areas that were located further in the countryside. He saw to it that criminals were prosecuted, and sometimes intervened when cases were decided on the basis of bias or personal grudges. Unlike many of the courts prior to his reign, he made far greater use of juries.

Another difficulty was the economy which had fallen into disarray during Stephen's reign. Henry encouraged the regrowth of financial institutions. Due to the reforms he set in place with regards to currency, trade picked up. A royal treasury was established monitored by an exchequer. Most of his income during the first half of his reign was from tax payments based on "demesne," or the lands owned by the English subjects. Other monies flowed from the payment of fines.

Henry generally had cordial relations with the Church, but did run into conflicts with church officials when the Pope attempted to have more control over the British than Henry did. A perennial battle with royalty occurred when popes made their own decrees bind members of a kingdom and Henry had strong feelings about his domination over ecclesiastical disagreements.

The Murder of Archbishop Thomas Becket

In 1162, Henry II appointed a good friend, Thomas Becket to the position Archbishop of Canterbury. As they were dear friends, Henry felt that he would prevail if the church issued a decree with which Henry disagreed. He was wrong.

If a cleric committed an offense, Henry felt it was well within his right to have them tried in a court of civil law. That is, they would be treated the same as a secular. Becket, on the other hand, insisted that priests be tried in Church courts by religious prelates.

In 1164, Henry passed the Constitutions of Clarendum, which mandated that clerics be punished for offenses to the same extent that criminals were. For example, in religious courts, a man could murder another and only be penalized by being defrocked. In a civil court, a criminal could be executed.

In essence, the penalties weren't really the pivotal issues. The governmental precepts represented a limit placed by the state over the church. It would set a serious precedent. Becket and King Henry also disagreed over the tax-free status of church lands and other state mandates. Their arguments became widely known, and people relished the gossip it instigated. What's more, other Church leaders became involved including Pope Alexander III.

Becket and Henry were both headstrong and stubborn causing the verbal war they waged to became increasingly nasty. Henry harassed Becket's friends in Britain, and Becket excommunicated people who supported the King on various issues that arose. Even when Pope Alexander III intervened, it was to no avail. Henry and Becket despised each other and misused their authority to win.

In 1170 CE, four knights approached Becket inside the sanctuary of his church to arrest him. Becket refused, saying it was irreverent to do that inside a church. The knights then brutally hacked him to death, leaving his body bleeding upon the altar rail. Thomas Becket was regarded as a hero by the people and by other European countries, his death cause people to lose respect for Henry II.

Rebellions threw England into Chaos

In 1169 CE, Henry invaded Ireland to solve a dispute with the King there. The Irish King made the error of hiring Anglo-Saxon mercenaries which set off ethnic hostilities between the Anglo-Saxons and the Normans.

In the meantime, the greedy British barons again rose up. So did two of Henry's own sons, Richard "The Lionhearted" and John Lackland. Henry appointed Richard as the heir apparent, but gave his youngest son, John three castles. John was his favorite. Because Henry was still living, Richard was essentially made powerless by his domineering father. In protest, Richard fled to King Louis of France for help. Matters accelerated when Henry went over with troops and initiated a series of battles. Soon the European countries, especially France, became involved in the controversy and all were at the brink of war.

While Henry was in France, King William of Scotland took advantage of the internecine war and attacked south England. English rebels in the North then became involved. As a ploy to lure Henry back to England, the Count of Flanders announced he was going to support the rebels and attack Britain. The ruse worked causing Henry to rush back to England. Henry captured King William of Scotland and imprisoned him along with a number of the rebellious barons.

Hostility raged on until 1175, when King Henry delicately negotiated with the various parties involved and made public reparation for the murder of Thomas Becket. He also pledged to go on a crusade to the holy land – a promise he never kept.

When a new king, Philip, rose to the throne of France, violence broke out between him and Henry. It took a year for Henry and Philip to call a truce which didn't last long as violence soon broke out again. In the end the pope had to intervene.

Henry then had difficulties with his sons over their inheritances, and he had to turn his attentions to home. Fighting broke out again between Henry and his sons, Richard and John. The stress of which proved to be fatal to Henry and he developed a bleeding ulcer. Henry II died in 1189. His son, Richard succeeded him.

Richard the ""Lionhearted"

Richard was called "Lionhearted" because of his military prowess. Even as a very young man, he wanted to participate in the Crusades, the efforts made to take the Holy Land from the Muslims. Shortly after Richard's accession to the throne, he went to the Holy Land. His brother, John, then took his place as regent to rule England.

King John

John Lackland was called "Lackland" because he literally "lacked land." Unlike other kings of England, he had very few estates of his own when he took power. Although he did have managerial ability, John was subject to much derision because of his nasty tendencies to be spiteful and petty. His older brother, Richard, was the popular son, not because he was a hero to his own people, but because he wasn't John.

His reign was tumultuous, and replete with a repetition of the revolt of the English barons who resented paying the taxes due on their huge properties. John needed the money for his military, because the nobles in northern France confiscated many of his holding in France. He assembled a coalition consisting of Otto II, the Holy Roman Emperor, Count Ferrand of Flanders, Duke Henry of Branant, duke of lower Lorraine, Count Renaud of Boulogne, and Count William of Holland, who never missed an opportunity to seize land.

John wasn't gifted with the ability to design effective military strategies and emerged from this without his inherited possession of the Duchy of Anjou.

"Pray for the Yeoman Named Robin Hood"

During the dark days of John, the king and nobles hunted in the royal forests first planted by King William of Normandy. The people also took the heavily shaded paths there in fear and trepidation of robbers everywhere. John heavily taxed his people, and ruled with an iron fist. During those treacherous days, a young rogue named "Robin Greenleaf," it is said, stole from the wealthy to give to the poor. According to one variety of the legend, he became an outlaw when he saw a poor person's last pennies taken from him to pay tax.

According to the "Geste (ballad) of Robyn Hode," Robin wasn't portrayed as a violent man. "Never use force," Robin would say to his band of merry men, "We shall do well enough; but look you do no farmer harm, that tills with his plow." However, when it came to wealthy bishops, Robin said, "ye shall them bear and bind; the high sheriff of Nottingham, let him not slip your mind."

Some historians differ, however. They indicate that Robin was a thief, as were many other displaced people of the time. He was more like a latter-day Jesse James, who sometimes showed compassion.

England was floundering in many ways and they needed a hero. Although the kingdom was united, it was united mostly in name only. Taxes were high, and the common people had to struggle through life, especially the peasants who were working on the estates for the barons.

The Magna Carta

Little by little, King John gained more power over the people, and became a dictator in essence. He prevailed even over the barons, and ran into disagreements all across the country and even with the pope, as he overtaxed the people and nobility. He had little respect for the rights of the people and even scorned traditional legal procedures when they were in opposition to his opinions. His will was law.

In 1215 CE, barons of the land spoke up for freemen everywhere in their kingdom and coerced John to sign the *Magna Carta*, which means "Great Charter." It contained precepts that protected peoples' rights. For instance, Clause 20 stated: "For a trivial offense, a free man shall be fined only in proportion to the degree of his offense, and for a serious offense correspondingly, but not so heavily as to deprive him of his livelihood."

The barons also made an attempt in the *Magna Carta* to grant freedom to the English Church.

John was manipulative and clever. He persuaded the pope to nullify the *Magna Carta* on the grounds it was coerced. His actions set off a fearsome rebellion by the barons who especially objected to John's obsession with regaining his lost duchy of Anjou, along with planning on a French invasion to take it back.

The Baron's War

The barons foolishly enlisted the aid of Prince Louis of France to put a stop to John's planned invasion. Prince Louis was thrilled at the opportunity. He stormed into Britain with his army and, in 1216, captured the important city of Winchester. Louis proceeded through England, conquering territory after territory. After he controlled half of Britain, he then demanded to be crowned king! Everyone saw through his empty boast, and no crown was forthcoming.

John retook Rochester Castle which had been seized by Louis and attacked the rebel barons. He then attacked the invader, Alexander II of Scotland who had allied himself with the rebels. He was actually able to drive the Scots northward toward Edinburgh. He snapped up the properties of the English barons on his way back south although their resistance continued. While the barons were wealthy, they were hard-pressed to pay all the military expenses for John's wars.

Not unexpectedly, even his military had mass desertions as everyone realized they were fighting their own countrymen to enhance the powers of a greedy king. Nature took revenge upon him on his way back. He had actually brought the crown jewels with him, but they were sucked up by quicksand at the edge of the marshes of the Wash – an area replete with estuaries. Half his baggage was swallowed up by the wetlands.

John suffered from chronic dysentery much of his later life, and died in the year 1216 CE. Rumors circulated that he was actually poisoned, but that was more the product of wishful thinking than reality.

Robert Bruce: Scottish Independence

The Kings had used Scotland as a playground for war over the years. During King John's reign, he invaded Scotland and actually made it as far as Edinburgh, which was an insult to the Scots causing them to become tenaciously united. Although they were Anglo-Saxons, they had Celtic roots and, in the 13th Century, most could speak Gaelic.

Balliol, the Scottish King, was under the thumb of the English monarch, Edward I. In fact, he considered Scotland a vassal state. The Scots were proud people, independent in their thinking and had a distinctive culture. In that sense, they were a minority, but one that should have equal rights along with Englishmen.

The Scots deposed the weak Balliol, and set up a committee of twelve to rule in his stead. King Edward had lost his power base in Scotland, so he imprisoned poor Balliol in the Tower of England and invaded Scotland in 1314. When the king died and was succeeded by a weak ruler, Edward II, Bruce sprung into action. "We fight not for glory, nor for wealth, nor honor, but only and alone for freedom which no good man surrenders but with his life," shouted Robert Bruce, one of the greatest leaders of Scotland. Although they weren't as well armed as the English soldiers, their sheer courage carried them through. The tight formations of the Scots, called, "shiltrons," broke up the English formations, and the Scottish cavalry was quite successful under the expert leadership of Sir Robert Keith.

The Scots won a stunning victory at the Battle of Bannockburn, and the English retreated. The Treaty of Edinburgh-Northampton of 1328 replaced the failed diplomatic Treaty of Arbroath of 1320.

Scotland was now an independent country.

CHAPTER 6 – "GREAT PITS WITH THE MULTITUDE OF THE DEAD"

The Black Plague was the great curse that overshadowed all of Eurasia. It struck in 1346 and raged on, carried from person to person, until 1353. There were so many dead, that bodies had to be buried in deep ditches and thrown irreverently into the ground to prevent further contagion. According to one of the Florentine chroniclers, "There were also those who were so sparsely covered with earth that the dogs dragged them forth and devoured many bodies throughout the city."

Peasants dropped dead in the fields they were plowing. Some blamed the Church; some fervent Catholics felt that God was punishing them for their sins, much like the prehistoric people felt that disasters were visited upon them by the deities. Others blamed the Jews, and accused them of polluting the drinking water. Many Jews were expelled from the towns and villages, beaten and tortured.

Symptoms were frightening. The ill were inflicted with uncontrollable vomiting, leading to the growth of black "buboes," or swellings under the skin. Nearly 50% of the population died. In time, the germ that caused this mutated into the pneumatic plague, causing incessant sneezing. The mortality rate of those infected then accelerated to 100%.

In those days, local churches used to keep track of births, weddings and deaths. However, the Church clerics themselves were dying. Consequently, many deaths went unrecorded. Today, when people trace their roots, many encounter large gaps of time, making it very difficult to determine one's ancestors during the 14th Century. Royalty had the luxury of moving to other castles where the plague hit less frequently. One never quite knew where the kings and their royal households were at times.

Ring Around the Rosy

There is an old nursery rhyme which is said to have originated during the Black Plague. In order to break the tension, and to alleviate the trauma of this horrendous disease, the children skipped around in a circle singing: "Ring-a-ring-a-roses, A pocket full of posies, A-tischoo! A-tischoo! We all fall down."
The roses and posies in the jingle refer to the beaked funnel-shaped mask worn by those who made the futile attempt of distributing herbs to ward of the disease. The funnel was full of those herbs. The sneezing referred to the uncontrollable sneezing that occurred shortly before the person died.

Causes

This was the bubonic plague, carried on the fleas of rats that infest the holds of many trading ships. When the fleas bit humans the disease was spread. Sanitation was very poor in feudal times. Grain was infested with rats, and when it was removed for food preparation, the people were exposed. In fact, waste water was thrown into gulleys on the dirt roads and little to no effort was made to remove horse defecation. People walking the streets did so at their own risk.

When the virus mutated into pneumonia, the death rate soared, as there were no antibiotics.

The Silver Lining

Those who did survive this terror actually had some benefits. Because there were less peasants to till the soil, wages became more competitive as the barons offered more money to peasants to work their fields, and improved their working conditions.

Taxes fell off significantly, as productivity decreased. For the first time in their lives, the commoners were actually able to bargain with their employers for higher wages and more suitable working conditions.

The Hundred Years' War

Since the reign of Edward III, which started in 1327, England had an ongoing argument with France over the French throne due to a questionable interpretation of old Salic law, the first law of succession in France. It was a complex but delicate issue, and seldom came up until there were disputes over the duchies English kings had claims to, specifically Anjou (which they were trying to reclaim since John I lost it), as well as Brittany, Flanders, Normandy, Touraine, Aquitaine and the city of Bordeaux. England and France also had disputes over the control of Flanders. Flanders was a vital market for English wool. In 1415 CE, Henry V the second king of the English House of Lancaster, resurrected the issue, and received quite a handsome settlement from the French. However, the English, for reasons most likely concocted, felt that France ridiculed the king and parliament then gave its assent to go to war.

Henry besieged the seaport of Harfleur and was successful. To demonstrate he had power over Normandy, he marched through there. However, he continued to march north and the French were obliged to stop them at Agincourt in 1415 CE.

The Battle of Agincourt

Many of the French soldiers were ill and desperately holding out for reinforcements. The French had a disadvantage due to the terrain on their side of the battlefield. Henry then caught many prisoners and executed them *en masse*. It was a disaster for the French, and they lost about 6,000 men, many of whom were well-known barons and dukes. By virtue of the Treaty of Troyes, he was awarded the right to succeed the current king of France, Charles VI. Before he could establish himself as King of England and France, Henry unexpectedly died of dysentery in 1422. As his son, Henry VI, was only an infant, France was placed under the regency rule of England.

The English made significant advances in France despite the French armed opposition. Then Joan of Arc emerged as the nation's heroine. Vigorously, she led her warriors against the English, defeated them at Orleans, and relieved an English siege there. By 1429, she and her army defeated the English at Jargeau and Patay. They then chased the English out of their holdings in France, when Charles VII won Normandy and Guyenne back from the English. Charles VII was then crowned king of France. England lost its holdings in France, except for Calais. The year was 1444. It wasn't until 1453, however, until Bordeaux surrendered which marked the end of the Hundred Years' War.

The War of the Roses

The "War of the Roses" was so-named because the emblem of the House of Lancaster was a red rose. The upcoming House of York was represented by a white rose.
Henry VI of the House of Lancaster, came of age back in 1437 CE assumed the throne. Through an arranged marriage, he wed Margaret of Anjou. Henry had serious bouts of mental instability so he was easily manipulated by Margaret and two powerful nobles, Humphrey, the Duke of Gloucester, and the influential Cardinal Beaufort, the 2nd Duke of Somerset. Through a series of machinations, Beaufort had Humphrey put into prison for treason where he died shortly thereafter.

Henry VI was unfit to rule, and Richard, the Duke of the House of York, became Henry's Lord Protector. He had Somerset imprisoned on trumped-up charges and effectively began to rule England.

The Duke of York was challenged by Queen Margaret, fighting for the Lancastrian cause, but she and her forces were defeated by Richard of York in 1455. Richard of York, with the aid of the Earl of Warwick, Richard Neville, kidnapped the disturbed King Henry. Boldly, Richard then claimed the English throne. Although Newville did have royal blood, his claim wasn't a strong one and was rejected by Parliament. They did, though, promise him he could succeed to the throne after Henry VI's death.

That issue became moot when Queen Margaret gathered up an army of Scots and attacked the Yorkists. Richard of York was slain in battle. After Margaret won the Battle of Wakefield, Margaret's son, Prince Edward would inherit the throne for the House of Lancaster. When Edward was full-grown, marched back toward London, they defeated Neville of Warwick and Henry VI was freed.

Queen Margaret then made a fatal error. Her army looted the countryside on their way to London and the Regency Council refused her admittance.

The Lancastrians Bide their Time

Warwick on behalf of the House of York allied himself with the Duke of Salisbury and the Earl of March, also named Edward. In the meantime, the Queen and young Prince Edward retreated to Dunstable, in East Britain. Warwick and the Earl of March entered London with their army in triumph. Warwick and Edward of March were popular in London and crowds cheered their entry. However, Earl Edward of March was determined to take the throne of England, but could not officially as long as Henry VI was the legitimate king.

The end of this horrendous conflict was near. Margaret, Henry VI and their armies were gathering strength to the east. To protect

Edward March's claim, Warwick likewise recruited armies to take on the Yorkists in one last glorious battle.

The Battle of Towton

This was the largest and bloodiest battle of the War of the Roses, involving about 50,000 men. It occurred in 1461 in Yorkshire in the middle of a blinding snowstorm. On the field of battle, Edward and the Yorkists let loose a massive volley of arrows that plunged into the bodies of the Lancastrian defenders aided by the bellowing winds in their favor. The Lancastrian archers were fighting against the wind, and snow blew into their faces, blinding them as they aimlessly shot back.

The Lancastrians then had their infantry charge forward ready for close combat. The Yorkists met them head-on with a wallop of bodies as they thrust upon the enemies. Suddenly the left wing of the Yorkists weakened and some of the men began to retreat as they faced death. Edward raced out in front of his men, beckoning them forward and they gained a second wind, fortified by his courage. The Yorkists then fought back, despite the fact that the Lancastrians outnumbered them.

Suddenly, the Duke of Norfolk, who had agreed to participate, showed up with reinforcements. Norfolk's forces attacked the left flank of the Lancastrians. They thrust spears and long knives into their foes bodies, and men from both sides fell in large numbers. The snow was red with blood and men slipped as they fell in the snow.

After three hours of grueling combat, the Yorkists won the battle. It was vicious and brutal. It was written that "bodies were notoriously left on the field." Archeologists reported that many bones of the dead which weren't recovered until the 15th century, were removed and reburied in churchyards, and some were later removed by an archeologist in 1907. They showed deep wounds to the stomachs and torsos of the soldiers. About 800 Yorkists were slaughtered, while between 3000 to 9,000 Lancastrians died. They had been exposed and abandoned to the ravages of nature for decades.

The unfortunate Henry VI, who had mysteriously recovered from his psychotic bouts, was imprisoned in the Tower of London, but they said he was well-treated out of respect. Margaret and the young Prince Edward were forced to go into exile in France, and they died impoverished.

Relieved by the end of the War of the Roses, Parliament approved the accession of Edward IV to the throne, and he was coronated in 1461.

Mysterious Disappearances of the Princes

Edward IV married Elizabeth Woodville from the power-hungry Woodville family. He wasn't supposed to marry her, as the Regency Council, the power behind the throne, decided he should marry Eleanor of Talbot. Edward and Elizabeth Woodville gave birth to two boys, Edward the V, heir-apparent, and his younger brother, Richard who was awarded the title Duke of York. Their uncle, Richard of Gloucester, was Edward V's Lord Protector.

Edward IV suddenly died in 1483, and the kingdom was thrown into crisis over the succession because the queen's relatives and Richard of Gloucester had designs of their own. The existence of the two princes interfered with everyone's power-grabbing urges. Because of Edward's promise to marry Eleanor Talbot, his marriage to Elizabeth Woodville was declared illegitimate. Edward V's claim to the throne was declared null and void, and the two boys were taken to the Tower of London. They were treated well for a while and contemporaries reported having seen the boys enjoying the gardens around the Tower. Then they disappeared, to this day, no one knows what happened to them, and it is suspected they were murdered.

The King in the Parking Lot

After the disappearance of the boys, who were only aged 11 and

9 in 1483, Richard of Gloucester was crowned Richard III of England. He was born under the shadow of suspicion because of the disappearance of the two princes, but no one had any information other than conspiracy theories about the matter.

In 1485, Richard III fought Henry VII, from the House of Tudor, at the Battle of Bosworth. He died in the battle and history recorded that he was buried in a royal tomb at the Greyfriars Abbey in Leicester.

He wasn't buried in an honorable way, probably because he was blamed for the deaths of the two princes, including the heir apparent, Edward V. Oral tradition is fraught with rumors, and people of the time said that after he was slain in the Battle of Bosworth, his body was irreverently thrown in the River Soar.

A Welsh poet, Gut'or Glyn, recorded that the Lancastrian soldier, Rhys Thomas "killed the boar (Richard III), and shaved his head." Word had it that the soldier used a halberd (a pike with an axe at the end) and thrust it through Richard's helmet. His body was recorded to have been buried at the Greyfriar's Abbey in Leicester.

Greyfriar's no longer exists. One of the kings who succeeded Richard, Henry Tudor (Henry VIII), angrily went through a period when he dissolved many of the monasteries. In truth, these monasteries had great wealth, from the donations of its patrons over the years. Because of his hatred of the Catholic Church, which he based on his own personal principles and desired, Henry VIII destroyed many these historic buildings between 1536 and 1541. Greyfriars Abbey was destroyed in 1536, and its assets deposited in the king's royal treasury. For years, the tomb of Richard III was lost.

In the 21st Century, the Richard III Society conducted a large research project and located Richard III's remains in a car park servicing the city council of Leicester. His remains were confirmed in 2013. As history reported, the back of his skull had been severed. He was buried without a shroud and appears to have just been shoved into a hastily-dug grave. He was reburied with a solemn ceremony at the Leicester Cathedral in 2015.

CHAPTER 7 – THE TUDOR ROSE WITHOUT THORNS

Finally there was a respite from the violent reigns during the War of the Roses. Oddly enough, Henry VII's emblem was a white rose superimposed upon a red rose, showing the people that the Houses of Lancaster and York were now united.

The Tudors were of Welsh origin. Henry VII defeated the infamous Richard III in battle and ascended the throne at that point, in 1485. It was a relief for the British that they Henry married Elizabeth of York. She was a quiet woman. Henry VII was a fiscal genius. Because of the War of the Roses, the English treasury was nearly empty. Although it didn't make him popular among the peasants, Henry raised taxes. However, he also raised taxes on the wealthy nobles.

Henry was a clever marketer, and hated by the competition. One of England's main products was wool, and Henry manipulated trade agreements so that the Netherlands could be squeezed out of trade profits. In 1506, Henry took care of Philip of Burgundy after a shipwreck and then manipulated him into buying alum from England instead of from the Netherlands. Alum was imported from the east and was used for dyeing wool. Henry's agreement was called the "malus intercursus," meaning "evil agreement!"

The Star Chamber

The Star Chamber was actually a secret room in the courthouse with stars painted on the ceiling. Henry VII and his successor, Henry VIII, used the room to meet with Privy Advisors and decide difficult or sensitive cases. It was originally intended to mete out fair verdicts to those who were "above the law" because of their money, power or influence. It was also intended as a sort of court of appeals or means by which a person could cut through bureaucratic restraints that prevented a just verdict.

However, Star Chambers could also be used to convict one's political enemies arbitrarily. That's often how Henry VII and Henry VIII used them. Henry VII used the Chamber to keep threats to his royal power in check and to wrest property from the the landed gentry without the benefit of a jury.

Henry VII passed the Laws in Wales Act in 1535 and 1542. That imparted equal rights to the Welsh landowners as the landowners of the rest of England. However, that was a double-edged sword. That required that only English, not Welch, be the official language used in legal documents. The Law forced the Welsh to surrender some of their ethnic identity. Furthermore, these acts deprived local Welsh courts in the "Marches," which were ill-defined territories between Wales and England, from trying their own criminal cases.

Henry VIII

Henry VII's son, Arthur, was earmarked to take over the throne. Arthur married Catherine of Aragon. However, Arthur died young at the age of fifteen. Henry VII was devastated and basically started to lose interest. He was succeeded by his younger son, Henry. Henry became Henry VIII. He married his brother's widow, Catherine of Aragon.

Despite his overweight appearance in portraits, Henry, as a young man, was very athletic and virile and was known to have many mistresses.

He and Catherine had two stillborn sons. When the infant, Henry, was born in 1511, he died seven weeks later.

In a search for glory and power, Henry initiated a war with France in 1512. His own sister, Mary, was married to King Louis XII of France. While Henry was in France, the Scots attacked yet in 1513, England defeated the Scots. In 1516, Catherine gave bith to a daughter, Mary.

Anne Boleyn was Catherine's lady-in-waiting and over time Henry began to notice her. He wanted her as his mistress, but she insisted on being married to him first. Henry tried to get a dispensation from the pope to do that, but was turned down. Henry argued that he had married his brother's wife (Catherine), which was against Church Law, and therefore his marriage to Catherine of Aragon was invalid. Catherine, however, indicated that her marriage to Henry's brother, Arthur, was null and void because the marriage had never been consummated – a likely possibility.

Catherine was now 40-years-old, and likely too old to give birth to a son. Henry was desperate, as he didn't want a female to succeed him. Thus, he ignored the pope's refusal to grant a dispensation, put Catherine in a manor home elsewhere in the country, and convinced the Archbishop of Canterbury, Thomas Cranmer, to marry him to Anne Boleyn. Catherine wasn't permitted to see her daughter, Mary, ever again.

Henry and Anne married in 1533. During the same year, Anne gave birth to a daughter, Elizabeth. In 1534, Henry passed the Act of Supremacy, making himself the head of the Church of England, by which he claimed wasn't under the jurisdiction of the pope. He also passed the Treasons Act, which stated that, if anyone refused to accept Henry as the head of the Church, they were guilty of high treason.

During that time, Martin Luther initiated the Protestant Reformation and founded the Lutheran Church, which also rejected the spiritual supremacy of the pope. Prior to that, William Tyndale published the Tyndale Bible, written in English. The thought of an English Bible horrified the Catholic clergy who insisted that the Latin Bible was the only valid one. People seemed to prefer the Bible in English, as they could now understand what was written. Clergy and royalty weren't able to "editorialize" and slant the content to suit themselves. The people of the kingdom weren't vulnerable to the subjective interpretations of the clergy any more.

Yet, there were others like Bishop Thomas More who were purists and felt that Tyndale's Bible wasn't an accurate translation at all. Vital words like "church" were altered to read "congregation," which More felt changed the entire meaning of the word. A "priest" was also called an "elder," implying that Holy Ordination was no longer necessary. In fact, Bishop More refused to attend Henry and Anne Boleyn's wedding ceremony, saying that is was sinful in the eyes of the Catholic Church. Another Catholic Bishop, John Fisher, felt the same way and made it known.

The Disastrous Years

Anne wasn't popular at court or among the influential officials of the time. She was believed to be a spiteful and arrogant person who constantly grabbed power whenever she had the opportunity. People disliked her so much that they called her the "king's whore." She even antagonized Henry's very powerful Minister, Thomas Cromwell. Because of her willful behavior, Henry himself was become angry and frustrated with her.

In 1534, Anne became pregnant. Unfortunately, she miscarried. The gender of the baby wasn't able to be determined, as it was in a very early stage of development. Henry at that time was under a lot of pressure. Even though he had himself appointed as Supreme head of the Church of England, people like the influential Bishop Thomas More spoke out against Henry's religious policies, and so did More's fellow bishop, John Fisher.

Henry VIII then ordered More and John Fisher to be executed and in 1535 had both of them decapitated.

In 1536, Henry was running low in funds for the Treasury. He noted that the Catholic monasteries were quite wealthy. Now that he had supreme power over religious law, he had monasteries dissolved one by one, and confiscated their wealth. Henry then put Thomas Cromwell in charge. Cromwell was able to reduce the bribery that had sneaked into the system through the years, and get more money to put into the Royal Treasury.
Coincidentally, one of those fated monasteries was the Greyfriars' Abbey, where King Richard III's body was discovered and exhumed at a much later date.

In 1536, Catherine of Aragon died. Henry was thrilled. Now, he could easily divorce Anne, believing not even the strict Catholics would object because he was now a widower. Henry even discussed the possibility of divorcing the troublesome Queen Anne with Thomas Cromwell.

Later in 1536, Anne was again pregnant. During the same year, Henry was badly injured in a jousting accident and almost died. Anne was traumatized by it and miscarried her baby. As it turned out, the baby was a male. Anne was near despair, as she had now lost the male child Henry craved.

Anne Boleyn's brother had been a candidate for a revered position, as Lord of the Garter. More members of the Boleyn family lost their places at court. Anne herself continued to be maligned and was even accused of witchcraft. Her brother was accused of having an incestual relationship with her, and other male friends of the Boleyn family were accused of having sexual relationships with Anne.

All of those men were executed, and on May 19, 1536, Anne herself was beheaded outside the Tower of London.

Henry married Jane Seymour in 1537. She gave birth to a male child, Edward VI. Jane Seymour, however, died shortly afterward of an infection related to childbirth. Although he was reported to have loved Jane Seymour Henry could barely wait to remarry, and in 1540, married Anne of Cleves. Although she was an attractive woman, Henry struggled to get on with her at first before having his marriage annulled. He quickly fell in love with another female courtier, Catherine Howard.   The same year he divorced Anne of Cleves he married Catherine Howard. As a matter of historical fact, Henry had his advisor, Thomas Cromwell, beheaded on their wedding day! To this day, historians don't know why Cromwell fell out of favor.

Off with their Heads!

Unfortunately, Catherine Howard wasn't a wise woman. She wasn't a virgin when she married Henry, and there were whispers around the court that she had another lover in the court – Thomas Culpepper. Then it was discovered that Culpepper wasn't her only lover. She had a prior affair with her secretary, Francis Dereham. In 1542, Henry beheaded all three of them!

War with Scotland and France

Henry had dreams of annexing Scotland, so he could be king of the British Isles. Henry knew military action would help him feel better after having yet another failed marriage. In 1543, he invaded Scotland. When the Scottish king, James V died, Henry tried to get his son, Edward, engaged to James' daughter. However, Parliament didn't approve of the union. Scotland and Henry were at war with each other – on and off – for eight years.

Henry also wanted to leave the legacy of having recaptured the English territory of Anjou that had been lost under King John Lackland. So he proclaimed war on France as well.

Marriage to Catherine Parr

In 1543, after winning the first major battle in Scotland – the Battle of Solway Moss – Henry came home and married Catherine

Parr. She wasn't as good-looking as Henry's other wives, and he is said to have often argued with Parr about religion.

Then it happened. Henry's jousting accident that he had suffered when was married to Anne Boleyn became severely infected, and festered until it became ulcerated. Doctors were able to stave off some of the pain, but there were no antibiotics in those days. Catherine Parr being a compassionate woman cared for him.

Henry became more moody as he became more ill. He also became quite obese, but clinicians today indicate he more than likely had a hormonal disorder that contributed to his weight gain. It was even necessary to use wooden contraption to lift him in and out of bed!

In 1547, Henry died. He had a magnificent tomb planned, but it was never completed for him. Therefore, he was interred and buried in Windsor Castle next to Jane Seymour – the wife he had always loved.

Wars and Poverty

The English people were poor with the exception of those who were large landholders. One feature that remains today and is often imitated were the building styles of Tudor homes. Oak, one of the finest woods there is, was used in construction and the decorative exteriors are the envy of people today.

The common folk, however, had difficulty securing work and many wandered the towns and villages. They had to avoid arrest, though, as it was illegal to be unemployed. Only the elderly and mentally disabled were allowed to beg. Therefore, there were, no doubt a lot of people who pretended insanity.

Fortunately, the Thames River was teeming with fish, so people were able to eat. Roads were muddy most of the time, and smelled of horse dung. The parish was the center of life and even became the local governments for towns and villages.

People drank a lot of beer and ale in those days and gossiped about life in the royal castles over drinks in their dark and dingy taverns or played billiards.

Public theaters were held in marketplaces, and that lay the ground for playwrights, like William Shakespeare in the next century.

Young King Edward

Henry VIII's son, Edward VI, took after his father and spent a great deal of money. However, he was forced to economize by the Privy Council. England's Lord Protector, Thomas Seymour, was Jane Seymour's brother and he used to embezzle money from the treasury and give it to young King Edward. When Parliament discovered that, his political enemies tried to have him convicted of treason, but that charge wasn't sufficient for the death penalty. Therefore, they used the Star Chamber, created by King Henry himself, and charged by virtue of an Act of Attainder, which was the cosmetic term for conviction without a trial. The unfortunate Seymour was beheaded in 1549.

Poverty Ended the Wars

The war against Scotland and France that Henry VIII started back in 1543 was finally over in 1551. By 1551, none of the countries involved could afford to continue, so it was over. No side had gained anything from the wars, although Scotland was still free.

Young King Edward was never a healthy boy. At age fifteen, he was extremely weak and his legs were severely swollen and painful. He died of tuberculosis. His last words were "I am glad to die."

Bloody Mary

Mary I, daughter of Henry VIII and Catherine of Aragon, rose to the throne in 1553. Her mother, Catherine, was Catholic. Therefore, Mary also was a fervent Catholic. Single-handedly, she felt she could reverse the Protestant Reformation. A period of terror raced through the country when she initiated bloody revenge upon Protestants who would not convert. They were flogged, imprisoned and burned at the stake. For example, on September 22, 1556, John Noyes, a simple shoemaker and constable in Suffolk, was dragged out to the stake and burned alive. "It is better," he said, "that you suffer for well-doing, than for evil-doing." His execution and those of 295 others were listed in the 1563 *Book of Martyrs,* by John Foxe. Because of her murderous rampage in the name of religion, Mary was dubbed "Bloody Mary."

In 1554, a huge rebellion broke out, triggered by Sir Thomas Wyatt, a political activist. England no longer wanted to be dominated by Catholic morals nor be subject to papal pronouncements. Anyone implicated in Wyatt's rebellion was thrown into the Tower of London. Mary was ruthless, so she also sent for Elizabeth, her Protestant sister. To protect her rights to the throne, Mary had Elizabeth relegated to house arrest yet in 1558, Mary became deathly ill and died.

CHAPTER 8 – THE LAST TUDOR: "I HAVE A LION'S HEART"

Elizabeth I, Mary's half-sister, acceded to the throne in 1558. Fear and trepidation rippled through England over the monarchy and religion. Although Elizabeth had been exposed to Catholic teaching, she was a Protestant, and much of England sighed in relief.

With the aim of quelling some of the religious rebellions in England, Queen Elizabeth passed the Act of Religious Settlement in 1559. She also had people in religious offices take the "Act of Supremacy," attached to that, by which they swore to adhere to the faith of the Church of England. Elizabeth proscribed the English Book of Prayer for all the people. She did have it modified, however, to suit some of the Catholics and Lutherans, so the doctrines didn't differ that greatly.

Religious prejudice wasn't reserved for England. It existed in Scotland, and even in some European countries as well.

The Webs They Weaved

In Scotland, Elizabeth's Catholic cousin, Mary Stuart, a Catholic, rose to the throne of Scotland, and became Queen of the Scots. The war between Protestantism and Catholicism was more dangerous in Scotland than in England. In fact, the Protestant reformer, John Knox, was recorded to have said, "That where women reign and papists have authority, there must be a need for Satan to be president of counsel." For her protection, young Mary Stuart spent her young years in France. She was then married off to Francis I of France by Francis's scheming father, Henry II. He also manipulated young Mary into signing a secret agreement to bequeath her right to the throne of England to France, if she died without an heir. The issue never arose, as Francis died shortly thereafter.

Mary Stuart fell in love with her first cousin, Henry Stuart, who held the title Lord Darnley. Despite the fact she didn't have a dispensation from the pope, they married each other. Elizabeth of England was furious, as Darnley also had royal blood and was a threat to Elizabeth's throne. Shortly afterward, Mary, Queen of the Scots, became pregnant and gave birth to a son, whom they named James.

Mary's marriage to a Catholic irritated the Scots, and each side drew up forces against each other. There were no real battles – just skirmishes. Rumors also circulated that Mary had relations with her private secretary, David Rizzio. Darnley then, or so it was reported, murdered Rizzio in front of Mary. Further, Darnley demanded that he rule as co-monarch. The marriage between Mary and Darnley eroded as result of his murder of Rizzio, and Darnley's increasing arrogance.

The Explosion
Early in February, 1567, Darnley was ill and stayed over at Kirk o'Field, a former abbey repurposed as a hostel for nobles. Mary visited him briefly and left. Then there was a mysterious explosion. Darnley was killed. The general consensus was that several devious nobles, including Mary's new lovesick suitor, James Hepburn, the Earl of Bothwell, led the conspiracy. Bothwell was charged with the murder, but machinations behind the scenes resulted in his acquittal.

Mary married Bothwell immediately afterward and the two

planned on regaining the Scottish throne. Mary's sister, Elizabeth, was shocked when she heard the news and wrote, asking how she could marry a man "who has been charged with the murder of your late husband."

Bothwell's Mummy

The Scottish were horrified about the murder of Darnley and Scotland split into two disputing parties over the marriage of Bothwell to Mary. He and Mary rushed to a more remote castle of Dunbar to hide out. Mary was pregnant by Bothwell, but miscarried shortly afterward. The lords of the kingdom signed a Bond against Bothwell. Mary visited Bothwell, and they had one last embrace. Then Bothwell fled to Denmark.

In 1567, Mary was imprisoned in Lochleven Castle by the Scottish rebels. Mary was presented with papers indicating that she agreed to abdicate the throne in favor of her son, James. In the words of Mary's own secretary, if Mary refused to sign the papers, "They were to take her from Lochleven, and, as they were crossing the lake, throw her into it." In fear of her life, she signed the document.

James was already in the hands of Protestant lords who saw to it that he was raised a Protestant.

Bothwell, in the meantime, was chased into Denmark, captured and imprisoned at the Dragsholm Castle. He was tied to a pillar and died there. In 1976, his mummified body was discovered and identified. His remains are the only non-wax figure on display at the Edinburgh Wax Museum. Tourists flock there to see it.

In 1568, Mary Stuart's Catholic supporters helped her escape from Lochleven Prison and she fled to Elizabeth in England. Elizabeth then had her imprisoned at Tutbury Castle. It was cold and damp there and not a comfortable place for Mary to live.

Elizabeth's Own True Love

Soon after she was enthroned, Elizabeth's childhood sweetheart,

Robert Dudley, rushed to her, as he had seen the treacheries that she was facing due to the hatreds kindled between the religious factions. She was flattered, and immediately appointed him Master of the Horse, meaning he would accompany her in her travels. That gave him the opportunity to protect her. Dudley, it was rumored, was a good-looking man about 6' high with "good features," or so his contemporaries said.

Dudley was a married man, but his wife died shortly after Dudley and the queen reunited. It was said that that his wife, Amy, "fell down the stairs," a notion that would arouse suspicions. Dudley didn't meet with the approval of Elizabeth's advisors, so she kept him on staff, but wouldn't marry him. Queens were rarely given the luxury of marrying those they loved.

Rumors erupted when Elizabeth boldly had Robert Dudley's bedchamber built next to her own. This coincided with a mysterious "illness" in 1561. Word had it that the "illness" caused her body to swell. Twenty years later, a young man claimed his name was Arthur Dudley and he was the illegitimate son of Elizabeth and Robert. Arthur was interrogated by Sir Francis Englefield, who said Arthur's claim amounted to nothing. Oddly, though, Arthur "disappeared" after that and was never heard from again!

Marry Her Off!

It was vital that the English nobles attempt to marry off their queens to suitable men, as that might entail opening up relations with another country, and the gentry had to be careful. They introduced Elizabeth to a number of suitors. The nobles introduced Elizabeth to Francis, Duke of Anjou in 1572. The Queen had a habit of calling him "frog," a derogatory term for the French. She didn't mean it that way, and he was amused, even to the point of sending her a frog-shaped earring! The people however didn't look upon it so charitably.

In 1579, they had Elizabeth meet with King Eric XIV of

Sweden, King Frederick II of Denmark and Archduke Charles of Austria. However, relations with the Habsburgs soured when they were gaining control over England's arch-enemy, Spain, so the Archduke was rejected by her advisors.

Elizabeth was willful and was a strong woman. She liked flirting with the suitors they sent her, but – in reality – decided she wouldn't marry anyone for political purposes. She once said "I will marry as soon as I can conveniently."

Drake's Circumnavigation of the Globe

Elizabeth's deceased sister, Mary I, had married Philip II of Spain. He had no right to the English throne by virtue of an agreement signed upon his marriage, but craved the throne nonetheless. He was favored among the Catholics, as a means to have Catholicism restored as the state religion. To undermine Elizabeth, Philip was said to have conspired to have Elizabeth assassinated. To retaliate, Elizabeth hired her friend, Captain Frances Drake, the well-known adventurer and privateer (pirate), to harass Spanish ships and rob them.

Queen Elizabeth also wanted to make history by exploring the Americas. Already, Christopher Columbus had discovered what he thought was India. Later on explorers discovered that there was a whole new continent lying between the Western World and the Far East. Elizabeth hired Francis Drake to harass the Spanish ships and claim some of the American lands for England.

In 1577, he set out, crossed the Atlantic, sailed south and went through what is known as the Strait of Magellan – a strait toward the southernmost tip of South America. It avoids going all around Cape Horn. The 19th Century writer, John Masefield described it thus: "Cape Horn tramples beauty into wrecks and crumples steel and smites the strong man dumb." It has been rumored throughout the years that Drake actually went around the Horn, but most historians deny that. Regardless, the passage all the way around Cape Horn is called "Drake's Passage."

Drake sailed all the way up the coast of South America and raided Spanish settlements as well as their ships. Spain had established huge colonies in South America including Santo Domingo – the island Columbus first landed on – Chile, Columbia and Peru and Drake attacked a number of them. In 1579, he attacked the Spanish Galleon, the *Nuestra Senora de la Conception*, and removed a treasure load of silver, which he brought home to Elizabeth. She was thrilled and in 1580, Drake was knighted.

King Philip was furious about the loss of the Spanish treasure, and planned an invasion of England with his formidable fleet, the Armada in 1588. These were heavy ships equipped with a multitude of guns. The European world called Philip's fleet "Invincible."
It wasn't.

Defeat of the Spanish Armada

The English man-o-war ships were more agile, and their guns had a longer range than those of the Spanish. England then allied itself with the Dutch Republic to help. Spain sent out its enormous Armada of 130 ships, and planned on sailing across the English Channel. While the Armada was attempting to go into their crescent-shaped formation, the English ships picked off the enemy ships at random. As they neared the channel, the English forced the Spanish ships to tighten up and the fleet was besieged by a collection of English fireships. When the Spanish trips tried to avoid them and meet up with their own allies from the Duchy of Pharma from France, Dutch "flyboats" blocked their access. Flyboats were huge cargo carriers, sometimes used in war. The English defeated the mighty Spanish Armada in 1588.

The Babington Plot

In 1585, Mary Stuart was transferred under heavy guard to Chartley Hall in Staffordshire, while Elizabeth's chief spy, Francis Walsingham, investigated a plot to assassinate Elizabeth and place Mary on the throne of England and Scotland. The chief conspirators were uncovered and identified as Anthony Babington, James Ballard and Mary Stuart herself! Mary wrote a coded message requesting the assassination of Elizabeth. Mary denied her guilt, but two of her secretaries were interrogated and attested to the truth. In the year 1586, all the conspirators were executed, including Mary who was beheaded at Fotheringhay Castle in Northhampshire.

Deaths of Dudley and Elizabeth I

Elizabeth's real love, Robert Dudley, who was then the Earl of Leicester, accompanied Elizabeth on her triumphant procession after the defeat of the Armada. He dined with her several weeks afterward. However, on September 4 of the year 1588, Dudley unexpectedly died. He left a letter for Elizabeth wishing that she have a long life and good heath, and added, "I humbly kiss your foot."

After losing Dudley and so many of her trusted friends and advisors, Elizabeth sunk into a deep depression. She died on March 24th, 1603. Elizabeth I was the last of the Tudors who left their mark on history.

CHAPTER 9 – THE EARLY STUARTS

With the death of Elizabeth of the House of Tudor, and the ascension of King James Stuart in Scotland, both England and Scotland were united into one kingdom. James was known as King James I of Scotland and James IV of England. Queen Elizabeth was always reluctant to go to war, and as a result left the treasury in a healthier condition than how she found it. Once the threats of international wars was at a low ebb, merchants were free to conduct trade throughout the area.

The nobles were relatively well-off, but not enormously wealthy. Yeomen worked the farms they licensed from the landowners. There were craftsmen galore. Literature thrived, especially with the rise in popularity of William Shakespeare's plays.
The poor they always had with them, but there were national provisions for them. The churches saw to it that their congregants donated to the poor people. Ever able-bodied men and women were required to work. The children of paupers were often sent to become apprentices for craftsmen.

Realizing the harm of open streets running with raw sewage, the English built a water system of clean water from reservoirs and a sewage process as well. In London, the merchants and gentry lived on the West side and the poor lived on the East side.

Religious Issue: The Main Plot, the Bye Plot and the Gunpowder Plot

King James I and VI of England, was raised as a Protestant. He had lost his mother, Mary Stuart, because of a religious controversy that triggered assassination plots. He lived through the cruelties endured by people of faith who had lost their lives simply because they had the "wrong faith."

James wasn't as tolerant as the people had hoped, so, in 1603, there were three plots to usurp James from his throne – the Main Plot, the Bye Plot and the Gunpowder Plot.

The Main Plot arose as result of papal efforts and those of Philip II of Spain, to have Catholicism restored in England. Not all of it had religion as its central motivation. Much of it was political. Under the guise of religious preferences, Henry Brooke, the Baron of Cobham plotted to replace King James with Arabella Stuart. Arabella was a Catholic and a direct descendant of the House of Tudor. Philip of Spain funded the plots in order to usurp James. The Habsburgs of the Netherlands were also involved, as they, too supported the Catholic cause and actually wanted to control the English regime.

The Bye Plot was planned out by Sir Griffin Markham, a Catholic, and Baron Thomas Grey. Grey wasn't a Catholic, but was a promoter of greater tolerance for the Puritans, a faction of Protestantism. The famous Sir Walter Raleigh was also implicated because he filled the role of courier to bring in funding from Spain to complete the usurpation of the throne.

The Gunpowder Plot of 1605 was another sloppy effort to have Catholicism restored. King James had the "Act of Supremacy of 1559" extended to include members of Parliament. By that act, those who held a seat in Parliament had to swear to uphold the Church of England.

The mastermind of the Gunpowder Plot was Robert Catesby, who was ostensibly a Protestant, but a Catholic at heart. There were many like that, called "recusant Catholics," who didn't attend the Protestant church services. Gatesby's co-conspirators included the well-known Guy Fawkes with whom this plot is most commonly associated.

At the opening of the Parliament in November 5, 1605, Fawkes sneaked into the cellar of the Parliament building and planted 34 barrels of gunpowder. Fortunately, the plot was uncovered when one Parliament member, Lord Monteagle was warned in advance not to attend that session. He, in turn, alerted the authorities. The gunpowder was removed and Fawkes was arrested.

The co-conspirator, Henry Cobham, was released due to severe illness. Griffin and Markham spent the rest of their lives in the Tower of London. Robert Catesby escaped with some of the other conspirators and attempted to sacrifice himself with some of the leftover gunpowder. It was wet, but when it dried out it was set afire by a spark. Catesby didn't perish, but was maimed for the rest of his life. Guy Fawkes was executed for his part in the Gunpowder Plot.

Sir Walter Raleigh, another conspirator, was quite well-known wasn't executed while Queen Elizabeth I was alive, as she favored him. However, he was later executed under King James in 1618.

American Colonies

King James chartered the Virginia Company to create colonies in America. In 1607, a group of hardy colonists established a settlement in the newly discovered country of America. The colonists had trouble with the local natives there – the Powhatan tribe, and the chief tried to kill the settlement leader, John Smith. He was saved by a lovely tribal woman named Pocahontas. Although some peaceful co-existence did ensue, there were continual hostilities. With the aid of Sir Walter Raleigh, the settlers grew tobacco which they traded with England.

Popham colony in Maine was established by the Virginia Company in 1607 and that was followed up by a settlement called "Somers Isles," later known as Bermuda. Another settlement, Henricus, was created in Virginia in 1611.

The English often came to escape the religious persecution going on in Britain. The Puritans arrived on the famous vessel, the Mayflower, and settled in Plymouth in 1620. Relations with the tribal nation and the Puritans was peaceful, and Plymouth was followed up by a number of other settlements in Massachusetts.

King James' Bible

In 1611, King James commissioned the publication of the Holy Bible in English. The 1611 edition contains 39 books of the Old Testament, 14 books of the Apocrypha, and 27 books of the New Testament. Although the Apocrypha was included it was not accepted as divine scripture but rather additional reading like a commentary. It has since been removed from the King James version to remove any confusion. Although it's been revised, and put into more modern English. The KJV is still used today by many fundamentalist Protestants although many refer to it as the Authorized Version rather than the King James version.

"Double, Double Toil and Trouble"

In 1623, the famous playwright, William Shakespeare, wrote those words in his play, Macbeth. Those were the words of two craggy-faced witches whom Macbeth encountered. King James had a morbid fascination with witchcraft and he actually attended witch-burnings when he visited Denmark prior to taking the throne of England.

James's son, Charles I, was the one who faced the "Double Toil and Trouble." The troubles visited England when the population began to question the manner in which their country was run. There was no long-term preparation for the union of the three sectors of the British Isles – England, Scotland and Ireland. When James assumed the throne, he had to rule all three. However, each segment was different.

The English Civil Wars

In 1642, a conflict arose between King Charles I and Parliament.

The military general, Oliver Cromwell, and his followers called "Roundheads" led a Parliamentary rebellion against the king. The Cavaliers, or Royalists, supported King Charles.

Battle of Edgehill

This battle, fought in 1642, occurred close to London. Prince Rupert, led the Royalist forces and the Parliamentarians attempted to stop the Royalists as they moved upon London. Rupert's cavalry attacked the Parliamentarians who appeared to be fleeing the battlefield. However, the Prince didn't return to the battlefield, as he should have, but went after their supply line and baggage train. The Parliamentarians who were on the battlefield hit the Royalist troops who remained full-force. It was hand-to-hand combat. However, most of the Royalists were behind the Parliamentarians and the outcome of the battle was inconclusive.

The Battle of Newbury

In 1643, the Royalists seized Yorkshire and its environs. Robert Devereaux of the Parliamentarians was marching toward Gloucester, but ran out of supplies and retreated toward London. King Charles then blocked his way there, and forced the Parliamentarians to do battle at Newbury. He underestimated their strength and the Royalists were forced to retreat.

Battle of Marston Moor

In 1644, the city of York was besieged by the Scottish and the Parliamentary troops. King Charles had his full complement of cavalry at this point, then marched north, leaving Prince Rupert there to put a halt to the siege. Oliver Cromwell was there as well and moved his own horsemen behind the Royalists who were battering the soldiers at the front lines. The Royalists were badly outnumbered and put up a valiant defense against Cromwell, but were defeated.

Battle of Naseby

At the village of Naseby near Leicester, England in 1645, the Royalist forces attacked first with cavalry and infantry attacking simultaneously. Initially, the Parliamentarians faltered and were driven off by the Royalists. When that happened, Commander Ireton of Cromwell's forces was unhorsed, and the Royalists moved nearly in bulk after the segment that was weakening. However, they left their other forces vulnerable. Only half of the Parliamentary forces were clashing, so their uncommitted troops moved in and outnumbered the exposed Royalist troops at the left and the rear. The Royalists were forced up a slope, and eventually were forced to disperse and retreat.

Siege at Newark

In 1645, King Charles and his forces marched north toward Oxford, while other Royalists attempted to defend the garrison at the Newark Castle in Nottinghamshire. Preparations had been made and the structure was well-fortified at its corners. The battle ensued when the Parliamentarian pincers swooped up from the South and the Scottish troops rampaged down from the North. They pommeled at the walls, destroying two of the corner structures. This was an incredibly long siege, lasting from November 1645 until May of 1646. The population was walled up inside the castle most of the time. The River Trent flowed to one side of it and only served to obstruct any escape by the Royalist forces when Colonel Poyntz of the Parliamentarians jammed it up. Muskets and cannons were used, and the cannonballs bore deep gashes in the castle walls. Illness grew when the food ran out and typhus set in. The civilians and soldiers were forced to kill and eat what horses they had. Then King Charles arrived, having been expelled from his attempt to recapture his mainstay fortification at Oxford. He had barely escaped after disguising himself. He was then taken by the Scottish troops there. They took him to the Parliamentarian commissioners. For months, he negotiated with them, promising money and such like. Negotiations proved unsuccessful.

Captivities

Charles was taken to Northamptonshire. The Parliamentarians, who favored Presbyterianism, supported disbanding the army, while another segment of the army were congregationalists, and wanted greater political freedom. As they tried to work out their differences, Charles was taken to Newmarket, then Oatlands and then to Hampton Court. Charles attempted to negotiate, but his efforts were again unsuccessful.

Secretly, Charles made an agreement with the Scots to invade England in 1648. Unfortunately, they were defeated at the Battle of Preston in Lancashire. Nearly 300,000 people had died during the English Civil War.

In 1649, King Charles I was dragged before the court at Windsor Castle and placed on trial. He was found "guilty of all the treasons, murders, rapines, burnings, spoils, desolations, damages and mischiefs to the nation, acted and committed in the said wars."

King Charles was beheaded on January 30, 1649. It was the first time in English history a king was executed. He was interred at Westminster Abbey in Windsor.

The Interregnum

Oliver Cromwell, the leader of the Parliamentarians, set up the Commonwealth of England in 1649. Although he called it a republican government, Cromwell ran it like a dictatorship. Cromwell called himself the "Lord Protector" of England. There was no House of Lords and representatives for the House of Commons consisted of elected members who had sufficient monetary resources to quality. Republican reforms were proposed, along with religious reforms. Church ministers had to be chosen by the people in the church community, but those considered unacceptable were rejected by an elected body of "ejectors."

The military was run by major generals, and they also collected taxes and acted as governors. That lasted only a year because people feared they might become too strong and dampen reform efforts.

Once the monarchy had been abolished, the new-found freedom the British felt stimulated the economy and the proliferation of the arts. There was time for leisure activities as well, once the war was over.

However, Cromwell's successor, Richard Cromwell, wasn't as effective an administrator as his father was. The military became a threat to the people, as they feared that the discontented Royalists and Parliamentarians would again go to battle. The military had little respect for Richard, and he resigned in 1659.

Talk circulated about a return to the monarchy, but any monarch was to have more restrictions on his power. King Charles I's son, King Charles II was in Europe during the Oliver Cromwell's Commonwealth period.

Monarchy Restored

In 1660, Charles II was invited to return to London as a king. The Parliament was re-established as it was before. Although it was Charles's preference to allow for complete religions tolerance, Parliament passed the Clarendon Code between 1661 and 1665. According to the Corporation Act of 1661, holders of public office had to be practicing Anglicans. Under the Act of Uniformity of 1662, office holders and even the clergy were required to use the Book of Common Prayer that Queen Elizabeth had recommended. The Conventicle Act, passed in 1664, forbade religious meetings to be held outside the church in order to prevent contamination from those with different religious viewpoints. Some of these practices were transferred to America. In fact, the famous Anne Hutchinson, who was an American Anglican colonist in Massachusetts was excommunicated from her church for holding "conventicles" in her home. The Five-Mile Act of 1665 forbade non-Anglican ministers from preaching within five miles from their original homes and churches.

The beleaguered English Catholics, who had sufficient resources, sailed across the Atlantic and, in 1634, created a Catholic colony in Maryland.

CHAPTER 10 – THE PLAGUE, THE FIRE AND CONSPIRACIES

Plague Revisits

The Black Plague, which erupted and subsided in the 14th Century resurfaced in 1665 in the east side Parish of St. Giles-on-the-Field. Medicine hadn't reached the level that it could effectively treat the Bubonic Plague. Even though more sanitation was introduced, it was insufficient to control the rats that carried the fleas with the disease.

Houses where the plague had hit were quarantined and marked with red crosses. The famous diarist, Samuel Pepys, who was the Secretary of the Admiralty under King Charles II, commented, "But, Lord, how sad it is to see the streets empty of people. People fear every door that one sees shut up lest it be the plague." At night, the corpses were buried in pits. Those who could afford it, left during those horrid months and the streets of London were practically empty, save for the poor.

The Great Fire of London

In 1666, the baker, Thomas Farriner, didn't finish quenching the fires from the furnace at his shop on Pudding Lane. The fire spread all through his shop, burned through his thatched roof and spread over most of the city. Looking out at London, Pepys said, "It made me weep to see it. The churches, the houses, and all on fire and flaming at once, and the horrid noise the flames made!" Crowding in the city was severe, and craft shops were full of combustibles. Overhanging upper stores, or "jetties" had been forbidden in the building code, but most builders built them anyway. The jetties tended to accelerate the conflagration, as did the dry wood of the tenement houses of the poor.

After the Civil War, many citizens still owned gunpowder which the flames caused to explode. A lot of it was stored by the wharf and flames shot out following the blast which hampered the escape of those who were trying to leave by boat on the Thames.

The king had men tear down houses to create firebreaks, but – as one Londoner said – "The fire overtakes us faster than we can make the firebreaks." The fire raged on for five days. The temperature was reported to have been 1,250° Celsius, or 1,520° Fahrenheit. Over 13,000 homes were destroyed along with 87 Churches and numerous government buildings.

The Rye House Plot

In the back rooms of the Rye House, a Hertfordshire mansion, Richard Rumbold, a veteran of the English Civil War, Robert West, a lawyer, Thomas Wolcott, William Hone, John Ayloffe, Josiah Keeling and the famous philosopher, John Locke. Locke was implicated only because he helped secure the meeting place. These activists were trying to plan the assassinations of King Charles II and James II, the Duke of York. Although Charles was an Anglican, James, the Catholic son of Mary, Queen of Scots, converted to Catholicism, and he was the heir apparent. Anti-Catholic hysteria was as high as ever due to the English fearing interference from the pope.

There were other convoluted twists to the motivations as well related to the agenda of the Whig part faction, subplots that were discussed by a number of other politically-motivated figures related to control of England and Scotland. The issue about an assassination had been discussed in many circles and taverns.

although some only played minor roles as they just were present at the talks.

In 1683, Josiah Keeling, an oil merchant, became concerned that he might be charged if news of this plot and sub-plots got out. Keeling himself wanted to escape any prosecution. However, he was the one who actually informed a trustworthy jurist and Secretary of State, Sir Leoline Jenkins, about it. As investigations ensued, more people were implicated in the Rye House Plot, and other plots against the government. They were Sir Thomas Armstrong, Henry Cornish, who was Sheriff of London, Elizabeth Gaunt, Algernon Sydney, James Holloway, Baillie of Jerviswood, Richard Nelthorpe, Richard Rumboldt, William Russel and John Rouse.

Robert West, claimed he wasn't involved in discussions about the assassinations; he was trying to provide arms for America. Thomas Walcott made a deal to confess if he was to get a pardon.

False Charges

As a result of the investigations, a dragnet was thrown out and many people were charged and convicted. Not all were guilty. Elizabeth Gaunt, for example, had nothing to do with the plots, but was burned at the stake. She was a member of a "non-conformist" religion (Anabaptists). Algernon Sidney was opposed to the assassinations, but wrote an essay questioning the divine right of kings. One of the judges in the court disliked Henry Cornish for turning him down for a promotion. There were others who were found guilty by association.

Outcome

Of the group, twelve were executed; two were pardoned. Ten were imprisoned; eight were imprisoned, of which one committed suicide in the Tower of London. Five others were tortured.

The Catholic King

In 1685, King Charles II died suddenly and King James II and VII of England attained the throne. He made a proclamation called the *Declaration of Indulgence* in 1687, granting freedom of religion to non-conforming Protestants, like the Presbyterians and to Catholics. His real intention wasn't just to put a stop to the religious wars, but to open up public offices to those of other faiths. James did, however, take a major risk by requiring that all ministers read the *Declaration of Indulgence* from their pulpits. Seven Anglican ministers adamantly refused and the angry king had them imprisoned in the Tower of London.

James had two daughters by his first marriage – Anne and Mary. Both were Protestants. His second wife, Mary Modena was a Catholic and had a son, James Edward Stuart, more popularly known as "The Old Pretender." The British were overwhelmed with apprehension. To make matters worse, King James dismissed Parliament as he wanted to establish an absolute monarchy.

The Glorious Revolution

The gentry were furious when the King obliterated Parliament. For both religious and political reasons, the nature of English government changed between the years 1688 and 1689.

In 1688, public officials and former members of the Parliament contacted William, Prince of Orange in the Dutch Republic. He was married to King James's Protestant daughter, Mary, over in the Netherlands. William was also Protestant. The nobles complained to William that England was in dire straits and needed him to come over. To protect himself, King James II assembled an army, but – wanting to avoid full-scale bloodshed – decided not to attack and fled to France. On his way, he threw the Great Seal of the Realm into the Thames. England then indicated that meant that James had abdicated.

As she was James's Protestant daughter, Mary was then made Queen and her husband, William, became the King.

War of the League of Augsburg

King William III of England co-ruled with his wife, Mary. In 1688, as soon as he was named King of England, William was drawn into the War of the League of Augsburg. France fought against the Holy Roman Empire, Portugal, Spain, England, Ireland, Scotland and the Dutch Republic and raged on for nine weary years. William led the forces of England, Scotland and the Dutch Republic. The result of that war were a number of territorial changes, most of which were on European soil yet some were in America.

Partial Religious Toleration

In 1689, King William and the Parliament passed the Toleration Act. It guaranteed rights to Protestants of faiths besides Anglicanism. It restricted the freedoms of Catholics, however. Parliament lobbied and also passed the Declaration of Right which limited the rights of monarchs. Succession to the throne was also settled, because it proscribed that, if either monarch died, the other would succeed him or her.

The Jacobites and the Williamite War

The Scottish Clans were the hardy Highlanders accustomed to fighting in the rugged crags and hills. They were the:

1. Clan Cameron
2. Clan MacKinnon
3. Clan Murray
4. Clan McLean
5. Clan Keith
6. Clan MacDonald
7. Clan MacKenzie
8. Clan Frasier

While exiled in France, James II obtained French support and came back to Great Britain to regain his throne. Because he had a great deal of support from Ireland, James and his French allies landed in County Cork. There was also a large Protestant contingent there as well – the "Ulster Protestants"– and they started arming themselves.

The Catholics who supported James were called "Jacobites," which is derived from the Latin term for "James" – that is, "Jacobus." They mostly lived in Scotland, but went over the Ireland to provide support.

The Battle of the Boyne

In 1690, King William and his troops landed in County Antrim. The two forces moved toward the River Boyne and they fought for control of the ford there. William's men forced themselves across the river to go after the Jacobite foot soldiers, driving them back and took possession of the town of Oldbridge. Then, when the Jacobite cavalry came galloping toward them, the Williamites had to hold back until their own cavalry came bounding into the battleground. Rounds of artillery and gunfire permeated. In short order, many of the Jacobites were killed. Thus, they were forced to retreat.

William then marched to Dublin and proclaimed victory. James moved his army to County Wexford, and sailed back to France. The Jacobites were horrified, and thereafter called him "Seamus a' chaca," meaning "James the shit!'

At Limerick and Galway, other battles continued, carried out under General Godert de Ginkel. The Jacobites lost both. The war then moved into Scotland, where the Jacobites redeemed themselves by winning the Battle of Killiecrankle.

However, the Williamite forces won a victory against the Jacobites in 1691. As part of a truce, King William offered pardon to the Jacobite rebels and required that they take an oath of allegiance to the King and Queen.

The Massacre of Glencoe

When the Parliament became aware of the fact that not all of the Jacobites had signed the oath, they wanted to make an example of them. In 1692, a British regiment was dispatched to the Highland village of Glencoe and started by blocking off exits from the town. The Jacobites then set up lines of defense. Captain James Drummond told the townspeople to swear the oath: "See that this be put into execution, without feud or favor, else you may expect to be dealt with as one not true to King or government."
Those who resisted were immediately shot. Most belonged to the Clan MacDonald. Thirty men were killed outright.

Sir Walter Scott, in his 19th century poem, wrote of it: "Long have my harp's best notes been gone, Few are its strings, and faint their tone…Till startled Scotland loud should ring, 'Revenge for blood and treachery'."

Queen Mary's Death and Legacy

Queen Mary died in 1694. Before she did, however, she proposed that she and her husband built a college in the New World – the College of William and Mary. It was erected in Williamsburg, Virginia, and still exists today. The town was reconstructed and consists of replications of buildings from the period. Wandering historical actors and actresses recreate the manners of the 17th and 18th Century. Houses and craft shops operate there as they once did during these times. Millions of tourists have visited there.

The United Kingdom

To resolve possible future problems with the religion of the sovereigns, the Act of Settlement was passed by Parliament in 1701, which restricted the throne to only Protestants. In 1707, the Kingdoms of England and Scotland united, giving birth to the United Kingdom.

King William died in 1702 and was succeeded by Anne, the daughter of King Charles II. She reigned for only five years.

CHAPTER 11 – "CARRY THE LAD THAT'S BEEN BORN TO BE KING"

Return of the Jacobites

After Anne, died, she was succeeded by George I. He was also related to the Hanovers of Germany. English sovereigns now heralded from the House of Hanover.

While the Jacobites supported restoration of the Catholic monarchs, there were political forces in England, not necessarily Catholic, like the Tories, who supported the principle of royal succession of hereditary monarchs.

The deposed king, James II, who was living in France died in 1701, but he had a son – James Francis Edward Stuart.

There were many skirmishes fought in Scotland over the restoration of the Stuarts. However, the Jacobites lacked solid military training, and there were frequent disputes among the different clans as to how to proceed.

The Highlanders called on the Old Pretender, James to return to Scotland and regain the throne. He came over in 1715, but rushed away after being defeated at two battles, and losing the support of the French. He was given sanctuary in Rome under the pope. The Jacobites were furious at his desertion to their cause, and called for his son, "Bonnie Prince Charlie" to come out of hiding and sail to Scotland. James Hogg wrote a ballad, "Come o'er the stream,

Charlie, dear Charlie, brave Charlie; Come o'er the stream and dine with MacLean." Charlie responded.

The Battle of Prestonpans

The English commander, John Cope, and his forces were in bad condition. He was much too sluggish in setting up his cannons in the little fishing village of Prestonpans, and, in 1745, Charles Stuart and the Highlanders took advantage and went after the British with their claymores, a two-handed sword. They hacked and slashed the English in a full-frontal assault. Highlanders were accustomed to the conditions and fought in the marshes, while the English got jammed up at one end of the long drawn out front line.

The Highlanders argued with Charlie who was focused on moving toward central England but his supporters wanted him to return to the Highlands. He acquiesced and in the same year, the forces marched toward Falkirk. They were followed by the English. The Highlanders men lay on their backs in the battlefield in the cold of winter. When the English horsemen galloped over them, the Scots cut into the bellies of their horses. When the enemies tumbled to the ground, the Highlanders stabbed them as they fell. It was bloody and brutal, but the Highlanders won. 500 British were killed or wounded. Many of them were slaughtered outright when they made a full-frontal assault, a move called the "Highland Charge." The Jacobites only lost about 100-120 men, who were killed or wounded.

The Siege of Carlisle

The town of Carlisle was occupied by the Jacobites earlier in 1745, but the government troops returned to take it back. The Jacobites only left about 400 men to man the garrison, when they moved on in England. The British commander, the Duke of Cumberland, hit it with heavy artillery. The Jacobites lacked sufficient numbers to endure this winter attack and had to surrender.

The Siege of Stirling Castle

In January, Prince Charles placed his Jacobite forces on Gowan Hill where they could fire on the government castle from higher ground. He had his men use sacks of dirt or wool to protect themselves from enemy fire. The transportation of the sacks slowed them down. The British Commander Blakeney opened with heavy fire, and it was very accurate. The British used mortar fire from the distance, but never mounted the hill because it was very steep. Charlie, in the meantime learned that the Duke of Cumberland was moving north of Edinburgh and had his men abandon the site.

Siege of Fort William

After having abandoned Stirling Castle, Charles and his men waited for Spring at Inverness. Then they got some support from France. Early on, the Jacobites blockaded the waterway for delivering supplies to the British troops. However, Commander Alexander Campbell sent in three boats of soldiers and killed the Jacobites there. The Jacobites put their guns on two hills overlooking the fort, but the guns weren't powerful enough to destroy its walls. Charlie tried moving in closer, but the British batteries were intensive. In the meantime, the British kept sending in units from their boats on the waterway. The Jacobites did penetrate some areas of the Fort, but only on the roof. Some of the British landing parties started damaging the properties of two Jacobite clans in the area – that of the Camerons and the MacDonalds. The siege went on for two weeks. When the Jacobite gun units were changing shifts, the British Commander, Scott, nearly destroyed their artillery. The Jacobites were then called upon by Charlie to withdraw to Inverness, and they had to forfeit the siege.

Battle on Culloden Moor

In 1746, British had assembled 12,000 troops. Artillery fire opened the attack, and then the left unit of Charles's line moved in and attacked the British Perth regiment. The Jacobite right flank moved in three units against the Atholl Brigade, and the Appin and the Lochiel units made their famous "Highland Charge."

After the charge, the Jacobite's left flank held back for too long before joining in causing the Jacobites to be divided. The moor was, as one would expect, muddy and the surface was slippery. Many horses fell along with the men, and the area was then drenched with blood as well as mud. Then the British opened up with musket fire, and the Jacobites struggled to get through the pile of dead bodies of both horses and men. They were then forced to flee.

The government forces increased in number and conducted operations on multiple emplacements of the Jacobites. They raided Lochaber where Donald Cameron was hiding out. Cumberland went after the MacDonalds at Shiramore and chased down Clan Mackinnon. Likewise, they raided their base at Inverness.

Battle of Loch non Uamh

In 1746, the Loch, or Lake, was loaded up with British ships, who engaged the French ships. The *HMS Greyhound* broadsided the French vessel, the *Le Mars*, and the French ship was destroyed along with its crew. The *HMS Greyhound* then attacked the French ship *La Ballone,* and the *Ballone's* mast was broken. The captain of the French ship, the *Baltimore*, sustained a head injury, and the rigging was shattered. A couple of French ships escaped along with the *Baltimore* which underwent repairs after the battle.

After the majority of battles had been won by the British, Charles Stuart took off into the western Highlands. His nemesis, the Duke of Cumberland chased him. Wearing disguises, Charlie made his way west, and hid out near the Hebrides with a woman named Flora MacDonald of the MacDonald clan. He was taken north by the MacDonalds and picked up by a French vessel, *L'Heureux*, near the Isle of Skye. Bonnie Prince Charlie was then taken to France.

The old Scottish ballad, the *Skye Boat Song*, told the tale of his escape:

> "Speed bonnie boat like a bird on the wing,
> Onward, the sailors cry.
> Carry the lad that's born to be king
> Over the sea to Skye.."

CHAPTER 12 – THE VICTORIAN ERA

The Industrial Era

Great Britain was considered the country that kick-started the Industrial Revolution. The invention of the steam engine was the result of the work of a number of inventors – Thomas Savery, 1698; Thomas Newcomen, 1712; John Roebuck, James Watt and Matthew Boulton. Each engineer improved on the engines of the former inventor. James Watt kept improving on his model and, by 1790, he mass produced a model used by flour mills, iron ore processing plants, cotton mills and the like.

Adaptations of the steam engine were used for manufacturing textiles – a boon to England which raised a lot of sheep. Daniel DeFoe, the well-known trader and prolific writer, said: "We are the most diligent nation in the world. Vast trade, rich manufactures, mighty wealth, universal correspondence, and happy success have been constant companions of England."

Trade

Great Britain had expanded gradually after the discovery of the North and South American continent, so the colonies they owned in the New World provided opportunities for trade. Islands such as Trinidad and Tobago, Barbados, the Bahamas, Leeward Islands, Jamaica and Bermuda. The British people had also received charters from the monarchs to establish colonies in mainland America. Trade flourished between England and America.

The American colonists wanted clothing made in England, along with tea and spices that the English were able to buy from the East. In return, America grew tobacco, rice in the south, and made manufactured goods. The islands in the Caribbean that Britain controlled had many sugar plantations and fields of cotton, although it depended upon slave labor to produce it.

To protect themselves, the English had passed the Navigation Acts back in 1651, requiring the American colonies to first ship any and all exports to England, before American could send goods to other countries. As the productivity of the colonies rose, anti-British sentiment also rose.

Rivalries Triggered Costly Wars

In the 18th Century, the rivalry of other nations over trade had its negative economic impact on England. In addition, smuggling was a critical problem, as privateers from all parts raided English ships and confiscated their exports. Governmental spending also increased during the 18th Century due to the Jacobite rebellions, the War of Spanish Succession in Europe, the French and Indian War in the British American colonies.

Britain felt the impact of these wars economically and raised taxes on the British colonies. That, in turn, instigated hostility by the British American colonies, as they found that the taxes were excessive. They resented the Navigation Acts, as they wanted to trade with the world freely. They also rebelled against the English imports, and even dumped tons of British tea into the waters of Boston. They also self-imposed an embargo on English products arriving in America, and many English merchant ships had to return to England with their goods unsold. The Americans then started to smuggle their goods abroad. They also objected to the fact that they had no representation in the British Parliament.

The American Revolution and its Effects on England

In 1776, the American Revolution broke out. Great Britain's

prime minister, Frederick Lord North, had his subordinate, Lord George Germain handle the strategy of the war. Britain achieved monumental victories in New York and Philadelphia initially, but France allied itself with America. French fleets arrived along with thousands of troops under the command of Jean-Baptiste de Vimeur,and the Comte de Rochambeau with the aid of the Marquis de Lafayette. To make matters worse, Spain joined in on the American War. Regardless, England seized control of Charleston, South Carolina while the Americans and their allies were focused upon the north. The British, however, were blockaded in Yorktown, Virginia by a huge American-French-Spanish force of both men and ships. In 1783, England surrendered.

The cost of the American Revolution was huge, and the national debt exploded. It was necessary for England to raise taxes in order to pay the war debt. Furthermore, trade was interrupted both during and after the war. The manpower needs to man the British army were great, and German mercenaries had to be hired and paid. The financial impact, however, was short-lived and England recovered sufficiently by 1785 – a remarkable achievement.

Politically, the English government was criticized for having lost the war, and many people who personally sided with America, felt that they had no say. A call went out for constitutional reform.

The Irish Rebellion

In 1798, the Irish rebelled. They were influenced by freedoms represented by the American Revolution. The British government required that only Anglicans could hold public office. Yet most of the population of Ireland was Catholic or Presbyterian. The Catholics and non-Anglicans did, however, have voting rights, but only if they owned property. The British government sent in troops and quelled it though not for long. The death toll overall was between 10,000 – 30,000.

Free Trade

Because of the benefits of England's industrial expansion, the country became engaged in worldwide trade. In fact, Great Britain supplied most of the manufactured products of France, Belgium, Germany and even the United States. Britain didn't charge tariffs on its colonies and trade increased significantly.

Acts of Union of 1800

In 1800, this act united Ireland with England and Scotland to form Great Britain. Thus, the country became the United Kingdom of Great Britain and Ireland. Most of the Irish were Catholics, and other Presbyterians. This act created the "Protestant Episcopal Church in England and Ireland, and confirmed the independent of the Church of Scotland. The Catholics, however, were just promised Catholic Emancipation. Ireland was ruled essentially as a colony of Great Britain.

Catholics had no voting rights until 1829 because they were prohibited from owning land.

Queen Victoria

Victoria , born in 1819, ascended to the throne in 1837. Victoria didn't get along with her mother, Princess Victoria of Saxe-Coburg-Saalfeld, of German ancestry. She was the first monarch of the House of Saxony. Her father died in 1820. Victoria's mother was very fond of the English comptroller, John Conroy and always asked him for advice. Victoria despised him. Likewise, she intensely disliked her mother's lady-in-waiting, Flora Hastings. When Flora developed an abdominal growth, people didn't realize it was a medical condition, and rumors flew about that she was pregnant. Victoria insisted that it was her nemesis, John Conroy, who had impregnated the poor woman. Flora was forced to submit to a test of her virginity, but it proved she was, indeed, a virgin. The English people then turned against Victoria.

The Queen, desirous of distancing herself from her mother, married her cousin, Prince Albert of Saxe-Coburg. Shortly thereafter, she became pregnant. It was well-known that she disliked infants. "An ugly baby is a very nasty object," she once said, "and the prettiest is frightful."

Local Government – Reform Act of 1832

The administration of government became more localized during the late 19th Century. It could no longer be handled only through a national government out of London with volunteers taking care of local matters. There were too many electoral seats in the House of Commons in England and Wales. This act gave a more balanced representation to the districts. Cities gained adequate representation. The vote was granted to landowners, tenant farmers, householders and shopkeepers. Prior to that, a district could have from 2 to 12,000 electors! Only men who paid a rental of £10 or more could qualify.

Early Assassination Attempts

In 1840, Victoria was only four months pregnant, when a mentally unbalanced young man, Edward Oxford, shot at her and Prince Albert in their coach. Oxford missed, but admitted the crime. Because he was deemed insane, he was committed to an institution and later sent to Australia under a new name. In May of 1842, a man named John Francis attempted to shoot her. Prince Albert said he was "a little, swarthy, ill-looking rascal." His pistol wasn't loaded, but he escaped. The entire city police force tried to hunt him down. Prince Albert and the Queen didn't want to live at Buckingham Palace until he was located. Prince Albert reported that, when they were in their carriage the following day, he looked with suspicion behind every tree and fence. Suddenly, a shot rang out. The security forces, who were close by, rushed at the man and he was arrested, convicted of treason and sentenced to death. Queen Victoria commuted his sentence, saying, "The feeling that he is to be executed is very painful to me." He was exiled from Great Britain.

In 1842, John Bean, a teen, just 17-years-old, afflicted with kyphosis (hunchback) drew a pistol from inside his coat pocket and fired at the Queen's carriage. A bystander grabbed Bean's arm and he missed. The police discovered that the gun was only loaded with tobacco! A dragnet was thrown out and every unfortunate hunchback was interrogated until Bean was found at home. He was taken into custody and sentenced to 18 months of hard labor.

The Potato Famine of 1845

The staple crop of Ireland was the potato. They had developed a wide variety of dishes with the vegetable, which grew well in Ireland. However, there was an infestation of *Phytophthora infestans*, a fungus. The Queen petitioned Parliament to repeal the "Corn Laws," which had raised tariffs on substitute vegetables. The laws were temporarily repealed, but it wasn't sufficient enough to compensate for the shortage. Tenant farmers were unable to grow enough other types of vegetables to feed the Irish and millions died from disease and malnutrition.

Queen Victoria donated the equivalent of about £6.5 million in aid. The British Relief Association also sent over donations.

Many Irish who could afford to, emigrated to America and Australia. The general historical consensus, however, is that Great Britain mishandled the crisis, and in 1997, Prime Minister Tony Blair made an official apology for the failing.

Another assassination attempt occurred as result of the famine. In 1849, William Hamilton, an Irish immigrant was out of work due to the Potato Famine. He shot a pistol at the Queen's coach but was apprehended by her guards. The gun only had powder in it – no bullet. He wanted to be put into prison where he would have prison work and food. He was sent to a prison colony in Spain.

Monarchical Revolutions

In 1847, Great Britain passed the Crime and Outrage Bill affecting a growing nationalist movement in Ireland. In 1848, the Young Ireland Party rebelled in Tipperary and the result of that was martial law. The rebellion was suppressed and leaders of the party arrested. Sporadic revolts occurred for another year.

These rebellions weren't restricted to Ireland, however. Uprisings occurred throughout Europe, and Queen Victoria and the Prince were moved to the Isle of Wight for their safety.

Fight with Lord Palmerston

Henry Temple, who had the title of Lord Palmerston, was the British Foreign Secretary. He had the tendency to make decisions without consulting Parliament, the Prime Minister, John Russell, or the Queen. Victoria was furious, as was the Parliament. In 1851, he took it upon himself to approve Napoleon Bonaparte's coup in France. In 1852, he and John Russell were replaced.

Empress of India

In 1857, a rebellion broke out in India, then owned and ruled by the British East India Company which was then dissolved. The Queen was disheartened by the rebellion and said that she had "feelings of horror and regret at the result of this bloody civil war." After that, India became a protectorate of the British Empire, with Queen Victoria as its Empress.

Two Royal Deaths

In 1861, Victoria's mother died and at the end of that year, her husband, Prince Albert died of typhoid. She went into seclusion after that, angering the populace. Victoria became ill in 1871, from an abscess, but the medical arts had reached the stage that she was treated and cured. Her son, Prince Edward, the heir apparent, nearly died of typhoid in the same year. After his recovery in 1872, Queen Victoria appeared again in public.

Two More Assassination Attempts

In 1872, a 17-year-old Irish teen, rushed at the Queen's carriage with a flintlock pistol. Her personal attendant, John Brown, tackled him to the ground and he was taken into custody. His alleged complaints had to do with the Irish famine, and he also apparently wanted prisoners to be released. He was tried, and found to be mentally ill. They exiled him to Australia.

It seems that would-be assassins always looked for opportunities to attack the Queen when she was in her carriage. In 1882, a 28-year-old young man, Roderick Maclean rushed toward her carriage when she was met by a group of cheering Eton College students. A shot rang out. The Eton students then rushed toward MacLean and pommeled the man with their umbrellas. He was subdued, and taken into custody. At his trial, it was determined he was insane and he was committed to a mental institution.

Late 19th Century England

Even though the Industrial Revolution created a new middle class in Britain, little was done to improve sanitation and safety in London itself. The city was overcrowded and toilets weren't emptied, leaving the city with a stench. Parliament established Boards of Health and passed new regulations that resulted in a safer building code. However, it took years before England could replace all of its slums.

The unemployed were forced into public workhouses, and children were separated from their parents. The poor called these houses the "Bastilles" after the infamous French prison.

Despite that, conditions started to improve, but gradually. Anesthetics were introduced to treat infectious illnesses. Photography was introduced and eventually became commonplace. Gas lighting was provided in London and major cities. More food became available as trade increased.

Queen Victoria's Death

Queen Victoria was one of the longest-reigning monarch in English history, having served as queen for 64 years. She had severe rheumatism and bad cataracts. She was staying at one of her preferred residences, the Oxford House on the Isle of Wight.

In January of 1901, she died and was succeeded by her eldest son, Edward VII.

CHAPTER 13 – BRITAIN AT WAR

Irish War of Independence

From 1912 to 1920, Ireland campaigned heavily for Home Rule. It was promoted by the Irish Parliamentary Party. Sinn Fein, a particularly violent splinter group, preferred a form of Irish Independence. The Ulster movement opposed Home Rule and rejected the plan that Ireland would be governed from Dublin.

The nature of the government in "Southern Ireland" was in a period of unrest because nearly all of the elected representatives in the Irish Parliament heralded from the extremist group, Sinn Fein. There were only four elected representatives that participated in the Southern Parliament which had been structured by the Government of Great Britain. Sinn Fein ignored the UK Parliament. Instead, it created an assembly called the First Dail.

Also known as the Anglo-Irish War, this conflict was fought between 1919 to 1921. It pitted the British governmental troops (Royal Irish Constabulary - RIC) against the Irish Republican Army (IRA) representing the Irish Republic. The RIC were stationed in garrisons, but local shopkeepers refused to sell them food and goods. In 1919, there were nearly a dozen RIC members killed along with several Dublin policemen. The British government proclaimed Sinn Fein segment and the Dail illegal. Irish volunteers attacked the property of the British government and killed John Milling who had arrested volunteers for unlawful assembly.

Workers went on strike in Limerick. Many transporters refused to carry in British troops. Miscellaneous attacks were carried on the IRA. Many of the government-backed forces of the Royal Constabulary abandoned their garrisons. Then the IRA burnt their posts to the ground.

To retaliate, British soldiers destroyed many Irish establishments. Within a year and a half of the eruption of violence, British forces raided nearly 40,000 homes, and arrested almost 5,000 people. The Sinn Fein mayor of Cork was shot dead.

The Government of Ireland Act of 1920 called for the separation of Ireland into two divisions – Northern Ireland and "Southern Ireland." Northern Ireland consisted of six counties in northeastern Ireland. Both divisions were under the umbrella of the Kingdom of Great Britain and Ireland. Southern Ireland was called the Free State.

Anglo-Irish Treaty

In 1921, Northern Ireland was given the choice to "opt out" of the Free State in Southern Ireland. Borders between the two states were then established. A new governmental structure was set up for the Irish Free State.

While the unrest started to subside in the south, it continued in Northern Ireland and often focused on divisions between the Protestants and Catholics. Rather than being a battle of religious beliefs, it stemmed from the restrictions placed on Catholics – either overt or otherwise – in terms of holding public office, and even caused a segregation of housing. These events, called the "Troubles" continued through much of the 20th Century.

World War I

This war, fought mostly in Europe, had been brewing for some time, as the countries had built up hostilities over various issues. It started in 1914 over the assassination of Archduke Franz Ferdinand of Serbia. There were basically two coalitions – the Triple Entente including France, Russia and Britain. – and the

THE HISTORY OF THE UNITED KINGDOM

Triple Alliance – including Germany, Italy and Austria-Hungary.

Other countries assisted one side or the other, until there was a huge number of forces involved. The United States entered in 1917, Romania joined up in 1916, followed by Portugal, Japan, China, Greece and others. Other monumental events occurred within some countries during that span of time. In Russia, the Tsar was overthrown and the Provisional Government was replaced as result of the Bolshevik Revolution. Following that, Russia became the Union of Soviet Socialist Republic, or, the Soviet Union.

The Formidable English Military

For years, England has been known for its Royal Navy. England was considered the Master of Sea. It has the largest Navy in the world. In the Battle of Heligoland Bight in the cold North Sea, the British fleet defeated the German light cruisers and torpedo boats. One of the German commanders, Leberechy Maass, lost his life when the flagship he commanded was sunk.

The Air forces of the British Isles consisted of the Royal Flying Corps and the Royal Naval Air Service developed new innovations that greatly aided in victory – wireless communication and aerial photography. After the war, they were combined into the famous Royal Air Force (RAF) known the world around.

The British Army was a voluntary force, and many of the soldiers had experience manning posts all around the British Empire. Often, the Army participated in what was called the British Expeditionary Force that operated specifically in France.
Patriotism and courage were the stuff of writers, but Siegfried Sassoon, was a soldier who lived through the war, and captured the brutal realities of battle. In 1918, at the end of World War I, he wrote, "Soldiers are citizens of death's grey land, drawing no dividend from time's tomorrows."

The Treaty of Versailles 1919

The Triple Entente coalition won the war in 1919. Negotiations led to the split-up of several countries which wanted to be freed from German domination – Hungary, Czechoslovakia, Austria and Yugoslavia. Germany was required to disarm, and make certain territorial concessions.

In addition, President Woodrow Wilson laid the foundation for the formation of the League of Nations, established as an international forum where countries might be enabled to resolved their differences without resorting to war.

The House of Windsor

In 1917, during the reign of Edward VII, the name "House of Saxony," of which he was the second monarch, was changed to the "House of Windsor" due to the anti-German sentiment following World War I. The name "Windsor" was derived from Windsor Castle. The castle was erected during the reign of William the Conqueror in the 11th Century.

The German Menace

In 1933, England reduced spending for the Royal Air Force. It was a poor year to do so, as Adolf Hitler, the boisterous Fuhrer, who once said, "I use emotion for the many and reserve reason for the few," invested a great deal of money into rearmament of Germany. It was a glaring violation of the Treaty of Versailles. Among the military advancements Germany financed was the *Luftwaffe* – a crackerjack Air force. They secretly trained new pilots and prepared for war.

Germany also built U-boats to patrol the waters in the Atlantic and North Atlantic.
Hermann Goring, an experienced World War I pilot, was made the National Kommissar and established the Reich Aviation Ministry. They trained in strategic and tactical methods for combat. Dive bombers were planned, as they could swoop down on cities and ships, wipe out enemy communications bases, aircraft facilities,

roads and railways as well as ground forces. Winston Churchill was out of public office at the time, but – as a politician and statesman – he kept a handle on political affairs. He was widely respected and made a speech warning about the upcoming threat the Germany posed, criticizing the government's reduction of military spending.

Chamberlain was Prime Minister in 1938, and when Germany annexed the country of Austria and Sudentenland, which was an area around Czechoslovakia, Chamberlain appeased Hitler by simply getting him to agree to conquer no more countries in Europe. Churchill was extremely alarmed by that. He spoke in the House of Commons saying, "the gravity of the events…cannot be exaggerated."

World War II

Germany broke its promise to Chamberlain in 1939, and invaded Poland. England and France immediately declared war on Germany. Churchill was then appointed the First Lord of the Admiralty. Meanwhile Joseph Stalin of the Soviet Union signed a non-aggression pact with Germany. In 1940, the Soviets also invaded Poland and divided it between themselves and Germany, agreeing to split up Eastern European countries they conquered. The Soviets tried to conquer Finland, but failed. However, they did get some territorial concessions. Then they occupied the Baltic States, and parts of Romania, which they merged into the Soviet Union.

The English colonies and protectorates, Australia, South Africa, New Zealand and Canada joined in with the United Kingdom, forming the Allied coalition against Germany.

In 1940, Germany invaded Norway and Denmark, which they occupied. Chamberlain resigned and the United Kingdom appointed Winston Churchill Prime Minister. What's more, Germany initiated a "blitzkrieg," or "lightning war." They then crossed a string of fortifications, called the Maginot Line, that

France had built during World War I. The line was ineffective against the tremendous influx of tanks, the Luftwaffe and artillery. Benito Mussolini, dictator of Italy, was impressed with Germany's speed and boldness and allies with Germany to form the "Axis Powers."

Germany then raged into France, destroying their defenses as they moved in. The Germans invaded the Ardennes, a heavily forested region of northern France, which the Allies thought was impenetrable. Henri-Philippe Petain, a general, was then appointed premier. England had some of their expeditionary forces and the Royal Air Force there to aid France. The RAF was very short of planes and pilots. England was then forced to halt those operations and evacuate France at Dunkirk. France was forced to surrender and signed an armistice with Germany. Petain was then relegated to moving the French government to "Vichy France," or southern France. Germany and Italy divided up France, and the Vichy Regime moved into a smaller area. Because the Axis Powers had been so successful, Hitler in his arrogance demanded that Britain surrender. Britain, of course, refused.

The Battle of Britain

Knowing that England had to strike and strike fast, Winston Churchill bolstered up the English with an invigorating appeal to their patriotism, saying, "…if the British Empire and its Commonwealth last for a thousand years, men will say, 'This was their finest hour.'"

The Battle began with German air attacks against British ports and convoys, and air bases in southeastern England. The British and Canadian air defense was divided into four groups to defend Britain. Two more groups were sent to the north to protect northern England and Scotland.

The German bombers were light-armed planes, and therefore were particularly vulnerable. Because of their victory in France and elsewhere, Germany had expected the British to surrender without a fight. They were wrong. The Allies gained control of the English Channel, preventing the German Luftwaffe from destroying English shipping.

The Blitz

The Luftwaffe furiously attacked Great Britain, especially London. They raided industrial centers and cities. Civilians shut off all the lights in their homes, and those who could, fled to air raid shelters. Nightly, there were bombings.

The air strikes went on day as well as night. However, the flying distance required from the German planes only left a limited time for bombing. The RAF beat them off, but the German Bf 109 fighters bombers had the advantage. In response, the British used their Spitfires which could overcome the Bf fighter planes.

By October of 1940, Germany withdrew. Hitler had planned on a full-scale land invasion in what was called "Operation Sea Lion," but cancelled that. As result of this monumental battle, the Germans lost nearly 3,000 men and 2,000 aircraft. The Allies lost about 1,500 men and 1,700 aircraft.

Operation Barbarossa

In 1941, Romania, Bulgaria and Hungary joined up with the Axis Powers. Germany invaded the Balkan countries which was then being occupied by the Soviets. Germany then attacked the Soviet Union. Stalin was utterly surprised by this turnaround. The Soviet Union then joined up with the Allies and entered the war.

The Soviet army wasn't prepared. They had tanks, but their air force was outdated. Within two months, the Germans got within 200 miles of Moscow. Hitler was intent upon annihilating the Jews in the Soviet Union and as many of the Communist forces as possible. They had the Einsatzgruppen, or specialized units, who penetrated the population, killing anyone they considered dangerous. They conducted massacres of Jews, civilians and state officials.

Once winter hit, thousands of German troops were immobilized by the cold. They didn't have adequate winter clothing or sufficient supplies. Many died of exposure, illness or starvation.

America and the War

Churchill had been pleading the United States to join the Allies in the war. In March of 1941, President Franklin Delano Roosevelt signed the Lend-Lease Act intended to supply the Commonwealth, France, China and the Soviet Union with material including military equipment and supplies to help in the war effort. China was included because they were already engaged in a war with Japan – the Sino-Chinese War– which had started in 1937.
However, it wasn't until Pearl Harbor, Hawaii was attacked by the Japanese on December 7 of 1941 that the U.S. declared war on Japan.

Great Britain declared war on Japan also in 1941, following its attacks on Malaya, Hong Kong and Singapore. In 1942, Japan invaded Australia. The Allies then worked together to defeat Japan. America suffered a string of losses in the Pacific. However, the Battle of Midway – an island in the Pacific – was the turning point.
Because of the war in the Pacific, America wasn't active in Europe until 1943. In 1943, the American and British troops defeated the Germans and Italians in North Africa. Mussolini and his government fell in the summer of 1943.

The Battle of Stalingrad

In 1942, when the weather turned warm in Eastern Europe, the Germans activated their forces in the Soviet Union. They were severely defeated by the Soviets at Stalingrad, and that represented a turning point on the front in Eastern Europe.

From November 1943 to March of 1944, the RAF bombed Germany and Berlin. Four aircraft bombing units joined in that attack in March.

Operation Overlord and Surrender

In June of 1944, thousands of Canadian, British and American troops gathered in southern England to stage a massive assault on the European continent. On June 6, the Allies sailed across the English Channel in overcast weather and invaded the Germans in Normandy, France. Then they pushed eastward.

Once that happened, Hitler turned his focus upon Europe. However, the Soviet troops moved into Czechoslovakia, Romania, Hungary, Romania and Poland, and won successful victories. Once winter hit again, the Allies bunched up their forces and encountered the Germans in the Ardennes. An eyewitness, a US Army soldier, Charles Sanderson, described it: "Did you ever see land when a tornado comes through? Did you ever see trees and stuff, twisted and broken off? The whole friggin' forest was like that."

With the continual bombing in Germany, the city was in utter ruins. Adolf Hitler himself had been hiding in his bunker throughout that time. On April 30, 1945, he poisoned himself with cyanide along with a gunshot wound to the head. His wife, Eva Braun, died from cyanide poisoning.

On May 7, 1945, General Alfred Jodel of the German High Command surrendered unconditionally.

War Ends in the Pacific

On August 6, 1945, the U.S. dropped an atom bomb on Hiroshima. Three days later, America dropped another A-bomb on Nagasaki. Japan surrendered on September 2, 1945.

Paris Peace Treaty and Treaty of San Francisco

Negotiations for the Paris Peace Treaty at the end of World War II lasted from July until October, 1946. The Treaty wasn't signed by all signatories until February of 1947. The United Kingdom, United States, Soviet Union, called the "Big Four," and other Allied

Countries negotiated with the Axis Powers, including Germany and Italy, along with some other smaller countries. Terms embraced war reparations, territorial adjustments, and minority rights. In addition, Italy ended its colonial empire, and there were border alterations agreed to affection other countries involved. Arrangements were made to exchange prisoners of war. Some, who were accused of war crimes, were handed over for trial.

The Treaty of San Francisco, signed on April 28, 1952, was signed between the Allied Powers and Japan. Three Soviet countries refused to sign it, and two didn't sent representatives – Yugoslavia and India. Italy wasn't invited. Due to disagreements over the nature and status of the governments of China, the People's Republic of China, Korea and Taiwan, they didn't sign the agreement at that time. Japan lost its position as an empire, and its borders were returned to what they were prior to the war. An International Military Tribunal was established to handle issues related to war crimes.

CHAPTER 14 – THE UNITED KINGDOM: POST-WAR CHALLENGES

After World War II, England, particularly London, endured hardships because of several factors: 1) necessity of rehabilitation after the bombing; 2) a need for financing to recover from the war; 3) the improvement of trade relations; 4) the modernization of industry; 5) economic aid due to an extremely cold winter; 5) a need for nationalization; and 6) the need for a National Health Plan.

Nationalization

In 1945, the Labor Party won the majority of seats in the Parliament. They laid out a plan to nationalize industries and services such as the Bank of England, the coal industry, steel industry, aviation, cable and wireless telecommunications, railways, trucking, canals and utilities.

The Marshall Plan

This plan, developed by the United States. was designed to help European countries to rebuild and become more prosperous after the expenses of the war. It offered help in modernizing industries in need of it, and improve trade relations. The United Kingdom received the bulk of the funds, in the form of low-interest loans, while France and West Germany received somewhat less, as did other countries.

The Princess Becomes Queen

Prince Albert was ill throughout the war, and eventually succumbed to coronary thrombosis and a heart attack. He died in February of 1952. Princess Elizabeth was then the Queen. She was then head of the countries in the Commonwealth – Canada, New Zealand, Australia, Pakistan, South Africa and Ceylon. Her coronation took place a year later – in June of 1953.

Queen Elizabeth is a constitutional monarch, but the power of the central government has devolved to grant powers to the Parliament. Scotland, Wales and Northern Ireland are self-governing bodies. Southern Ireland, is a sovereign state and a republic. Canada is a constitutional monarchy where the executive powers reside in a cabinet, ministers of the Crown, responsible to the House of Commons and led by a Prime Minister. New Zealand is also a constitutional monarchy with a parliament. In their constitution it is written, "The Queen reigns, but the government rules." Australia is a federal parliamentary constitutional monarchy. The Queen is represented by a Governor General. The Falkland Islands, are a self-governing overseas British territory and the monarchy is the head of state. Pakistan is an Islamic republic under a constitution. After the secession of "East Pakistan," it became the "People's Republic of Bangladesh," an independent Parliamentary Democracy. Like Pakistan, it is no longer under the English sovereign. South Africa is parliamentary republic, independent of an English Sovereign. It is run by an elected President. Shortly after World War II, Ceylon, or "British Ceylon," achieved independence and became the country of Sri Lanka. It is a democratic socialist republic with a President and Prime Minister.

The Queen is married to Prince Philip, the Duke of Windsor. The heir apparent is Prince Charles, her eldest son.

Economy

By 1950, Great Britain bounced back full-force. The standard of living increased. Unfortunately, after the next ten years, England couldn't maintain that level of growth and plunged into an economic downturn. Much of the cause of that was due to a global recession and stagflation in England. The term "Stagflation," invented in 1970 by the British conservative, Ian Macleod, occurs when inflation is high, but the rate of economic growth slows down or plateaus, and the rate of unemployment remains high.

The "Iron Lady"

One of the contributory factors that created the state of stagflation is an increase of the money supply in an atmosphere of a slowing of economic growth. It creates inflation. Margaret Thatcher lowered the inflation by increasing interest rates. She also raised some taxes, and cut public spending starting in 1979. Although she was highly criticized for that, Britain showed signs of economic recovery in 1982. Following that, unemployment fell, and the economy started to stabilize.

One of the main ingredients for what became known as "Thatcherism" was the privatization of industry and state-owned utilities. The Parliament passed regulations to curb the growth of monopolies. The British Steel Corporation, for example, was able to made tremendous profits, even as a state industry. The privatization introduced encourages competition, which – in turn – led to price reductions. She didn't favor universal privatization. With regard to the British railway, she once said, "Railway privatization will be the Waterloo of this government. Please never mention the railways to me again."

Falklands War

In 1982, the country of Argentina invaded the Falkland Islands, the islands of South Georgia and the South Sandwich Islands, all of which lay just off the eastern coast of Argentina, claiming those islands rightfully were Argentinian properties.

Britain immediately sent out a naval task force, submarines and the infamous RAF, which engaged the Argentinian Air Force and Navy, later following it with an amphibious landing.

In April the Argentinian submarine, *ARA Santa Fe* was spotted by a British helicopter near South George Island, and the helicopter dropped depth charges. Two anti-submarine helicopters, Westland Wasps and the Westland Lynz launched torpedoes using their specially-designed guns. Along with antiship missiles from the *HMS Endurance they* damaged the submarine, and it was unable to dive.

A British force was disembarked backed up by a naval bombardment. The RAF sent out the Vulcan Bomber and bombed a runway at Stanley, the capital of the Falklands. That prevented Argentina from flying jets from the airbase. Four more raids followed that one, and the Argentinians withdrew its Mirage III fighter jets to Buenos Aires.

Argentinian aircraft were shot by British Sea Harriers, airplanes that could take off and land vertically. One of two Argentinian Mirages was shot down and another limped back to its base, but was destroyed by friendly fire. Then a British submarine sunk the Argentinian battle cruiser.

Then the Argentinian Naval Air Fighters attacked the *HMS Sheffield* destroyer, killing 20 crew members. Due to fires, the ship was abandoned and sunk. An amphibious landing was made. The town of Goose Green was subdued by the British commandoes and they moved on to San Carlo. They were unsuccessful, after being shot at by Argentinians Skyhawks.

The British then engaged in night attacks at three sites near Stanley and took away Argentinians positions on the high ground. Then the Scots Guards captured Mount Tumbledown and defeated the Argentinian defensive forces near Stanley.

In June of 1982, the Argentinian commander, General Mario

Menendez surrendered to Major General Jeremy Moore.

"George, This Is No Time to go Wobbly"

Those are the famous words of Margaret Thatcher when the U.S. President George H.W. Bush hesitated in making the decision to pull together a coalition to eject the Iraqi President, Saddam Hussein from Kuwait which he attacked and occupied in 1990. The coalition consisted of Kuwait, the United States, the United Kingdom, Saudi Arabia, Egypt and France. The United States, the United Kingdom, Saudi Arabia and Egypt provided the largest bulk of forces for this, the Gulf War.

After being preceded by heavy coalition artillery fire, the British armored forces were the first to move into Kuwait and they were followed by the Americans. The two divisions targeted Saddam Hussein's Republican Guard. The fighting was intense, but the coalition pushed Hussein's army back into Kuwait City.

The Kuwaiti's came storming in afterward and started liberating the city. The Iraqi's offered only light resistance, but hit the coalition troops hard at the Kuwait International Airport. Four days later, most of the Iraqi's withdrew.

Then coalition forces invaded Iraq with the U.S. 2nd Armored Cavalry Regiment and that was accompanied by a simultaneous airborne attack. Another U.S. armored cavalry regiment and infantry troops, supported by a French army division went storming in. The U.S, 101st Airborne Division attacked behind enemy lines further west, and effectively cut off the Iraqi supply lines. The Iraqi's started to retreat further westward.

The French forces engaged the Iraqi infantry in their effort to prevent an Iraqi counter-attack, and their right flank was supported by the United Kingdom's Armored Division. Many Iraqi tanks were destroyed. The British attacked Iraqi's well-known Medina division and overcame them, destroying more Iraqi tanks and capturing an Iraqi general.

The Iraqi troops who remained behind in Kuwait set fire to a number of their oil fields, and the sky rapidly filled up with blinding black smoke.

In retaliation, Iraq hit Saudi Arabia with SCUD missiles. Hussein also sent in SCUD missiles to Israel. The Coalition then spent much time on the ground hunting down and destroying what SCUD missile bases they could locate.

In February of 1991, Iraq surrendered agreeing to withdraw from Kuwait and recognize its sovereignty.

Iraq had suffered extreme losses. Nearly 50,000 Iraqi's were killed, while the coalition only incurred 292 deaths.

Before the Kuwaiti War was over, Thatcher came up short of the 15% majority needed to run for re-election. Another balloting could have been done, but her Conservative advisors convinced her to resign. She was replaced by John Major.

CHAPTER 15 – WHERE ARE THE WEAPONS?

After the war in Kuwait, Iraq was required by the United Nations to eliminate its weapons of mass destruction. Iraq didn't fully cooperate with inspections performed by of the International Atomic Energy Agency (IAEA). In 1998, Saddam Hussein ceased his cooperation with the inspectors.

The Iraq Liberation Act of 1998 was passed the U.S. Congress and President Bill Clinton signed it into law. The statement made supported efforts for creating a democratic government in Iraq.

Operation Desert Fox

This was a four-day bombing campaign manned by the United Kingdom and the United States to strike military targets associated with the production, maintenance, and delivery of weapons of mass destruction, including biological, chemical and atomic weapons, and related research facilities.

In December, British aircraft flew missions to take out on 97 targets. The U.S. fired missiles that struck six of Hussein's presidential palaces, Republican Guard barracks, and other military targets. They were assisted by the Royal Airforce, using their Tornado aircrafts. 11 weapon production and/or storage facilities were taken out by cruise missiles and bombs.

Operation Telic: The Iraq War

"Operation Telic" was the British code name for its military participation in the Iraq War. The Iraq War, fought between March 2003 to December 2011, was a pre-emptive strike by a coalition consisting of the U.S., the United Kingdom, Poland, Australia and Peshmerga. Peshmerga is an autonomous Kurdish state lying within the borders of Iraq.

Part of the initial invasion was intended to find weapons of mass destruction. Among the items found, were aircraft buried in the sand! In addition, there were toilets and guns made entirely of gold!

Operation Telic was one of the largest British deployments ever engaged after World War II. 64 British warships along with mercenary merchant vessels, an aircraft carrier named the *HMS Ark Royal*, the British 1st Armored Division, three army brigades, the Royal Marine Commando Brigade, a mechanized Division and the RAF were engaged. Rear Admiral David Snelson was the Royal Navy commander.

The United Kingdom was based in the city of Basra, Iraq. After 2007, England essentially left, although there were some clean-up operations they conducted. They left Iraq in 2011 – the same year the U.S. also left. Participation in the Iraq War was and is a highly debated issue in England. Some say that the Prime Minister at the time, Tony Blair, had been misled by American Intelligence which claimed that weapons of mass destruction were present in Iraq. None were found.

The invasion resulted in the occupation of Iraq and the establishment of a parliamentary government under a Shia Muslim government, which was hotly disputed after the war.
Tony Blair was succeeded by Gordon Brown, who indicated in that the United Kingdom never saw any of the American Intelligence reports, and that the conclusions drawn were based on imprecise judgements and assumptions, not hard evidence.

That was followed up by the Chilcot Report, an inquiry completed in 2011 conducted by Britain into the necessity for military action in Iraq. It concluded that Saddam Hussein didn't pose a sufficient threat to justify such an invasion. The Prime Minister at the time, David Cameron, said that Britain and the parties involved should reflect on "the lessons of what happened and what needs to be put into place to make sure that mistakes cannot be made in the future."

Boris Johnson is the current Prime Minister. He heralds from the Conservative Party. He has taken steps to increase public spending, including more money for the police and public education. His government has a "pro-China" policy and encourages an open economy for the two nations that would stimulate Chinese investment. To promote free trade, Johnson supports the Chinese efforts to establish overland routes, after the example of this historic Silk Road. That would entail efficient transportation systems, and is extended to mean that maritime routes would also be developed. This is called the Belt and Road Initiative.

The United States has lodged its objections to that, implicating that there is a hidden agenda attached to it. The U.S. feels that such a project might lead to Chinese global economic domination.

CONCLUSION –

The United Kingdom has traveled the centuries and held its head high among the strongest countries of the world. After its fascinating beginnings as a motley group of disparate ethnic groups from the North Sea, it has emerged as one of the most adaptive and modern countries in the world. The major countries of today's world actively seek out the opinions of British leaders and politicians.

Like so many of the European countries, Britain's early days were marred by the internecine struggles that peppered its succession of hereditary monarchs. It is a country whose early history was punctuated with plots, conspiracies, assassinations, love triangles and the stuff that sometimes has a way of sounding like gossip columns.

Yet, despite the avarice of dictators, and all the failings that make people human, the British have overcome that and become one of the greatest nations in the world. Even foreigners know the patriotic songs, *God Save the Queen* and *Rule Britannia* and sing them with zest.

Britain is a country that respects its past. Everywhere in the British Isles historical buildings and monuments have been preserved and attract thousands of tourists annually.

AFTERWORD

Thank you for reading about the history of the United Kingdom.

Our goal is to make history informative and enjoyable without blocking up our books with filler. If you have enjoyed this book please leave a rating or review, it allows others to know you enjoyed the book.

You can also visit our website below and sign up for our newsletter where we include offers and news of new releases.

History Nerds Newsletter

Made in the USA
Las Vegas, NV
30 November 2024

e87ee163-7539-46f0-9aaf-50422222a01dR01